WWF

World Wildlife Fund

TAKE ACTION

An Environmental Book for Kids

by Ann Love and Jane Drake

Illustrated by Pat Cupples

Tambourine Books
New York

Inquiries should be addressed to Tambourine Books,
a division of William Morrow & Company, Inc.
1350 Avenue of the Americas, New York, New York 10019.
Printed in the United States of America.

Library of Congress Cataloging in Publication Data

Love, Ann.
    Take action / by Ann Love and Jane Drake; illustrated by Pat
Cupples. — 1st U.S. ed.   p.   cm.   Includes index.
    Summary: Discusses the importance of nature, the threats to
various animal and plant species, and what young people can do
to help protect the environment.
    1. Nature conservation—Juvenile literature. 2. Endangered
species—Juvenile literature. 3. Environmental protection—Citizen
participation—Juvenile literature. [1.Conservation of natural
resources. 2. Wildlife conservation. 3. Rare animals. 4. Environmental protection.] I. Drake, Jane. II. Cupples, Pat, ill. III. Title.
QH75.L68   1993   333.95'16—dc20   92–30412   CIP   AC
ISBN 0-688-12464-X. (lib.) ISBN 0-688-12465-8 (pbk.)

10 9 8 7 6 5 4 3 2 1
First U.S. edition, 1993

TABLE OF CONTENTS

WILDLIFE MATTERS   6

Why should you read this book?   8
Wildlife — who needs it?   10
Imagine a world without...birds   12
Out on a limb   14
Extinction is forever   16

ENDANGERED SPECIES   18

Don't shoot   20
Spot the wildlife products   22
Blow the horn on wildlife trade   24
Food poisoning   26
Bad news numbers   30
Balancing the numbers   32
Wildlife close-up: the whooping crane   34
Jet set eggs   38
Mr. Whooping Crane   40
Success stories   42

ENDANGERED SPACES   44

Wilderness — who needs it?   46
Wildlife and people — uneasy neighbors   48
What's wild in the west?   52
Timberrrr!   56
Clear-cut victims   58
A spill to cry over   60
Acid rain — the silent killer   64
Temperature rising: the greenhouse effect   68
Wildlife close-up: the rainforest   70
A tropical rainforest in your home   74
Rainforest action file   76

HOW TO TAKE ACTION   78

Kids can make a difference   78
On your own: a wildlife-friendly lifestyle   82
In a group: more wildlife-friendly ideas   86
Glossary   92
Index   93
Answers   96

ACKNOWLEDGMENTS

The exciting ideas and activities of the following teachers, parents and kids have made this book possible:

Dawn Allen, Jeff Andrew, Graham Angus, Ken Arnott, Michael Arsenault, Marise and Simone Arsenault-May, Danielle Balineau, Lyn Baptista, Andrea Barnett, Fran Barnett, Gregory Barnett, Tim Beatty, Cathy Bell, Johnathon Bendiner, Cathy Black, Renee Bouthot, Todd Brandt, Edie Brewer, Allison Eddy Brown, Maria Brunati, Teresa Buchanan, Phillipe Buckland, Nelleke Calder, Judy Chambers, Joyce Crebase, Stacey Danchuk, Lada Darcwych, Jacobus de Bock, Paul Delong, Derek Derkson, Walter Donovan, Brian Drake, Madeline Drake, Stephanie Drake, Eleah Elstone, Andrea Evenson, Kristina Farr, Peter Fenton, Marla Fine, Deborah Fisher-Tubb, Shauna Flanagan, Jenny Franco, Linda Fury, Kathleen Gaudi, Larry Geer, Jane Golding, Mary Granskow, Marilyn Greenlaw, Alicia Griffin, Eve Gruss, Michael Guglietti, Peter Hall, Heather Hansen, Dina Hanson, Jill Hermant, Christopher Hinley-Smith, Melinda Hofer, Jean Horne, Brian Irving, Barbara Jamieson, Shane Jeffrey, Jodi Kalbflesh, Karen Keagle, Tara Keir, Heather Keith, Sarah King, Francine and David Knight, Karen Kosten, Sarah LeBlanc, Adrian Love, Jennifer Love, Melanie Love, Greg Marshall, Kayvene Martin, Lewie Miya, Jane McConnell-De Cirso, Nancy McGhee, Audrey MacGregor, Stacey McGuckin, Rebecca MacKinnon, Charles McLaughlin, Erin Meilleur, Jacqueline Millage, Scott Mills, Sarah Morrison, Matthew and Ben Oleynik, Greg Ollerenshaw, Elizabeth Parry, Melissa Parsons, Carolyn Pearce, Stephanie Piehl, Mary Pitblado, Maria Price, Alison Riddle, Michael Robson, Daun Rose, Helen Roulston, Kira Rowat, Mari Rutka, Gerda Rykert, Judy Sartor, Kyla Schmed, Barbara Seiler, Sandy Shaw, Shelley Shaw, Marion Shynal, Katie Skead, Margaret Skinner, Karen South, Jessica Stam, Flickerine Stevens, Stephanie St. John, Anna St. K. Greg, Jessica Stratton, Barry Stroud, John Trueman, Troy Tyndall, Cass Van Eisinga, Colin Vernon, Amanda Walsh, Melanie Watt, Dawn Webley, Krista Wheildon, Amy White, Alicia Willis, Tina Winter, Shirley Ann Wipf, Susanne Wobschall, Elgin Wolfe, Jennifer Wouk, Tanya Yeoman and Corrina Yuen.

Particular thanks to the students who evaluated the activities in this book: Cathi Bremner's 4 – 6 Enrichment Class at The Country Day School, Judy Davenport's Grade 6 class at Walter Scott Public School, Pat Davis' Grades 2–3 class at Whitney Public School, Whitney School Interest groups, Students of The Bush School Elizabeth Taylor's Grade 6 students at E.J. Sands Public School and Bob Sandiford's Grade 7 students at Roselawn Public School.

The authors acknowledge the Canada Life Assurance Company whose support of *Operation Lifeline* allows many young people to take action to help save wild animals and wild places.

The authors also gratefully acknowledge the professional advice and assistance of Elizabeth Agnew, Ian Barnett, Joe Bird, Kathleen Blanchard, Margaret Chrumka, Jane Crist, Jim Drake, Stephen Johnson, JoAnne Joyce, Keith Kavanagh, Ernie Kuyt, Gary Linglen, David Love, Elizabeth MacLeod, Peter Martin, Edward Pembleton, Michael Perley, Steven Price and Randy Saylor. Thank you also to Valerie Hussey, Ricky Englander and the staff at Kids Can Press. We are especially grateful to our editor, Valerie Wyatt, for her good-humored guidance and encouragement!

The writers dedicate this book
to our parents, Kathleen and Henry Barnett,
whose lifelong love of nature and science
is a constant inspiration.

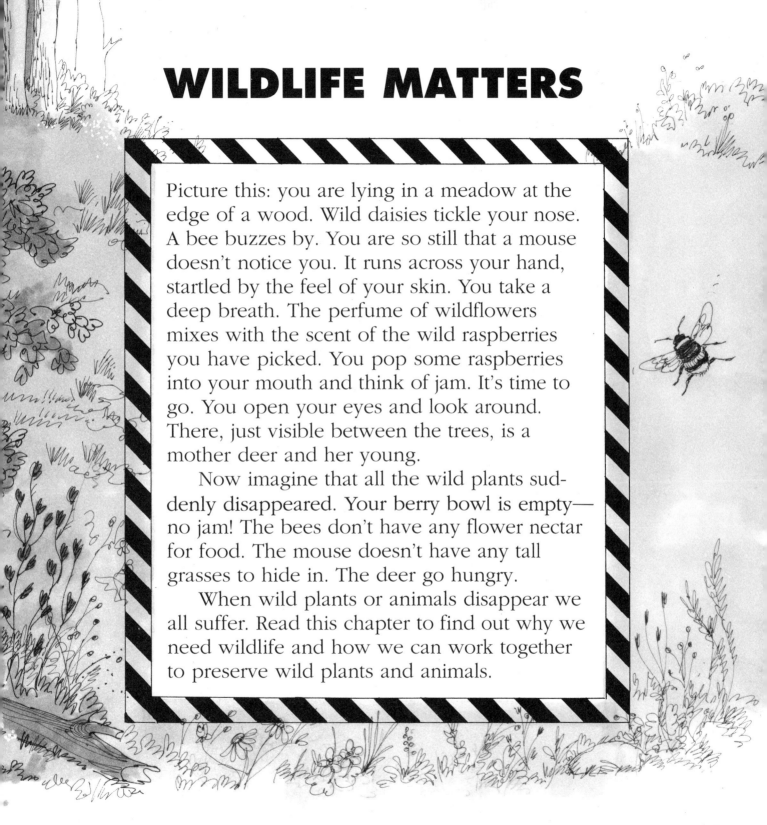

WILDLIFE MATTERS

Picture this: you are lying in a meadow at the edge of a wood. Wild daisies tickle your nose. A bee buzzes by. You are so still that a mouse doesn't notice you. It runs across your hand, startled by the feel of your skin. You take a deep breath. The perfume of wildflowers mixes with the scent of the wild raspberries you have picked. You pop some raspberries into your mouth and think of jam. It's time to go. You open your eyes and look around. There, just visible between the trees, is a mother deer and her young.

Now imagine that all the wild plants suddenly disappeared. Your berry bowl is empty—no jam! The bees don't have any flower nectar for food. The mouse doesn't have any tall grasses to hide in. The deer go hungry.

When wild plants or animals disappear we all suffer. Read this chapter to find out why we need wildlife and how we can work together to preserve wild plants and animals.

WHY SHOULD YOU READ THIS BOOK?

Wild animals and plants need your help. Many species are in danger of disappearing from the face of the earth. Why is this happening? They are being poisoned by pesticides, killed by hunters, and their homes are being destroyed by cities that gobble up wild areas like monsters in a video game.

The destruction of animal homes, or "habitats," is the most serious threat. Every minute of every day somewhere in the world, people destroy animal habitats when they cut down forests for paper and lumber, plough up prairie grasslands for farms and spew pollution into the air that ends up in lakes and rivers.

Today many wildlife species are in trouble. In the United States alone, 462 plant and animal species were endangered in 1991. In Canada, 42 species were in trouble. These plants and animals will become extinct unless something is done to help them.

Fortunately, things are being done, and you can help. How?

Start by understanding what's happening. In this book, you'll learn how the passenger pigeon disappeared, why the right whale may be doomed and how the Indian tiger has been saved from extinction. You'll learn what wildlife species will be lost if we keep spraying pesticides on our forests and farms, filling the air with fumes from our cars and destroying the tropical forest at a rate of 50 acres (20 ha) a minute. You'll see how people rely on the variety in nature — for food, medicine, industry and life itself. You'll understand why, as the earth loses its diversity of wildlife, all living things lose out. Every time a species becomes extinct, it's eliminated not only from the present but from the future, too.

Once you understand the problems, pitch in and help. You'll get great ideas in this book from other people concerned about wildlife. Read about the kids from Winnipeg, Manitoba, who worked with seniors to plant a tall-grass prairie habitat and created beautiful gardens that provided homes for birds and butterflies. Find out how the students in Tenakill, New Jersey, stopped their school cafeteria from using Styrofoam. Look at the report on the students in England who staged a jungle walk art show and raised $108 to help save the rainforest.

When you've finished reading, decide what action plans you can start on your own. Talk to family and friends about joining your efforts. Try to get everyone around you involved in working to save wildlife!

What's It Mean?

WILDLIFE:
all wild animals, plants and wild places.

HABITAT:
the natural environment of an animal or plant.

SPECIES:
a distinct kind of animal or plant, such as a mallard duck or a green frog, that mates and has young with another of the same kind.

IF YOU STUMBLE ON A WORD YOU DON'T KNOW, LOOK IT UP IN THE GLOSSARY ON PAGE 92.

WILDLIFE — WHO NEEDS IT?

What would happen if a Malayan pit viper slithered into your kitchen? Your dad would scream, your grandmother'd faint and you'd run for your baseball bat, right? Before you finish off your unwelcome visitor, stop for a minute. The pit viper's venom makes a drug that helps prevent heart attacks in people.

Many wild animals and plants that you might consider creepy, ugly or annoying are valuable. Like the pit viper, they provide much-needed medicines or food for us and for other animals. And all plants and animals add to the variety and beauty of the earth.

The wild world is a rich and important natural pharmacy. Open your family's medicine chest and you'll probably see a bottle of aspirin or similar pain killer. Did you know that the ingredient that takes away

headaches comes from the bark of a riverside willow tree? Aspirin can be made synthetically using the chemicals found in the willow, but the heart drug digitalis can be made only from the real plant, the foxglove. Thousands of heart patients owe their lives to this delicate plant. Many hundreds of wild plants and animals contribute crucial ingredients to medicines. Wildlife saves human lives!

Without wild plants we wouldn't have food to eat. Today's food crops are all related to wild plants. About 3000 plants are eaten by people but only seven provide most of our food: wheat, rice, corn, potato, barley, sweet potato and cassava. What would happen if one of these "big seven" was wiped out? Huge numbers of people might become sick or starve.

To prevent this from happening, farmers can crossbreed farm plants with their wild relatives that are immune to many diseases. By protecting *wild* plants, we can keep our *food* crops healthy and preserve the world's future food supply.

Plants and animals also serve as food for other plants and animals. Mosquitoes might drive *you* nuts, but they're food for many amphibians and birds. Scientists see all living things as part of a large natural workshop called an ecosystem. Each creature or plant, no matter how small or ordinary we think it is, plays a vital role in this ecosystem.

The disappearance of one plant or animal can have serious consequences for others. Take the dodo tree and the dodo bird, for example. The dodo tree, whose fruit was the main source of food for the dodo bird, dwindled in numbers when the dodo bird became extinct. Then, with only 13 trees left in the world, an American scientist, Dr. Stanley Temple, discovered why. The dodo tree depended on the dodo bird to eat its seeds. The dodo bird's powerful digestive system cracked open the seed cases so that when the seeds were expelled in the dodo's droppings, they could sprout and form new dodo trees. The two kinds of dodos were interdependent; when the bird became extinct, the tree was threatened with extinction, too.

Not all plants and animals are as useful as the pit viper, foxglove and dodo bird. Some are just plain beautiful. People enjoy watching or photographing them. Wildlife enriches our lives and makes the world a more interesting place.

The One-Stop Plant

The winged bean of Southeast Asia has been nicknamed a "supermarket on a stalk" because almost all of the plant is edible. The leaves are like spinach, the young pods like tender green beans and the young seeds taste like peas. Fry the flowers and they taste similar to mushrooms. The tubers or roots can be boiled or fried like yams. Even the seeds can be crushed for oil or ground up to make a coffee-like drink. Talk about useful!

IMAGINE A WORLD WITHOUT...BIRDS

The dodo bird became extinct 300 years ago. Since then, many other bird species have disappeared forever. But what would happen if *all* birds became extinct?

RRRING! goes the alarm. It is 7:00 a.m. on a spring morning in the year 2000, in the town of Anywhere, North America. You open your eyes and strain to hear the morning chorus of birds. No cheerful call of the cardinal or chirps of sparrows. The slippery nylon comforter on your bed feels cold against your skin, not cuddly and warm like the down quilt you used to have. Tossing it aside you get up, thinking of breakfast.

In the kitchen, your mom is putting out cereal for you.

"How about eggs?" you ask.

"Sorry dear, I just can't get them at the store any more."

Stuffing your peanut butter sandwich in your lunchbox, you suddenly remember what a chicken sandwich used to taste like, with lots
of mayonnaise. Remember the goose at Christmas? The chicken nuggets at the take-out?*

Sports news comes on the radio and your ears prick up. The Toronto Domers trounced the Baltimore Blasters. Baseball was a lot more colorful when the birds were up to bat.

When you open the back door, you see that your brother took your bike, leaving you his, with a flat tire. What a turkey. Oops, haven't seen a live one of those for a while.

Better get ready to run to school. What's the rush? Take a look up in the sky. It's black with mosquitoes, flies, wasps and other insects. Without hungry birds to keep the insects under control, there's been an insect population explosion. If you want to get to school in one piece, you'd better run for it.

When you stop to think about it, birds play an important role in our lives. Food, feathers, song, color and enjoyment are just a few of their contributions to people. For bird-eating animals such as foxes and hawks, birds are even more important. If all the birds became extinct, many animals would starve and become extinct too. Birds — life just wouldn't be the same without them.

What if all the plants died? Or if every insect was wiped out? Imagine no wolves or whales. We need wildlife.

Would Life Be Fowl Without Our Feathered Friends?

Some birds are terrific rodent catchers — better than a mousetrap.

Who needs a fly swatter? One bird can eat thousands of insects per day.

Some birds are a walking restaurant for humans, hawks, foxes and many other animals.

Scavenger birds such as vultures are nature's waste disposers.

Spectacular colors and songs make birds a thrill to watch.

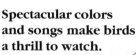
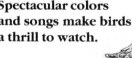

Winters are warmer with feather duvets and jackets.

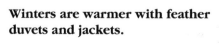

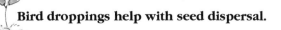
Bird droppings help with seed dispersal.

The Miner's Canary

Miners used to take caged canaries deep into coal mines with them. When a canary fell off its perch and died, the miners knew the air was poisoned with coal gas and they'd better get above ground — fast. The canary was a "bio-indicator," indicating to the miners whether the air was healthy enough for them to breathe.

Ducks were recently used as "bio-indicators" in Hamilton harbor, Ontario. The Canadian Wildlife Service put a flock of eight ducks into the harbor. The next day, seven were dead. That sent a clear warning that the water was seriously polluted.

Other species can also signal trouble. When trout disappear from rivers and lakes, we know the water is low on oxygen and high in silt. Clams are used to test for toxic (poisonous) metals in water, and certain types of grass indicate a high metal content in the ground. Trees indicate the air and soil quality in cities. Malformed leaves and dead branches show the tree is struggling to survive.

If wildlife is in trouble, so are we. What will happen if we don't listen to their cries for help?

OUT ON A LIMB

It's not likely that you'll wake up one morning and find all the birds gone. That would be a real disaster. But sometimes one species of animal or plant gets in trouble and starts to disappear.

Scientists, conservation groups and governments keep close tabs on wildlife to prevent this from happening. When they find a plant or animal that's in trouble, they put it on a special list so that everyone knows it's time to get working on a solution. The endangered species list has seven categories: extinct, extirpated, endangered, threatened, vulnerable, downlisted and delisted.

Dodo

Dodos were large flightless birds with no enemies — until the 1600s, when European sailors landed on the islands where they lived and started hunting them for sport. Later settlers brought along rats, pets and pigs, who ate the birds and their eggs. Dodos were extinct by 1680. Extinct means a species is gone, every last one of them, forever.

Many other plants and animals are extinct, such as New England's sea mink, Europe's auroch (a wild ox) and the Mauritian ebony tree.

EXTINCT

Eskimo curlew

Known as dough birds because they were plump and tasty, Eskimo curlews were over-hunted until their numbers fell from millions to about 20. Today, there is only one breeding colony left in the world, and its whereabouts in the Northwest Territories, Canada, is a secret. Eskimo curlews are listed as endangered: there may be too few of them left to carry on the species.

Other endangered species are the aurora trout and the cucumber tree. The swift fox has become extirpated. This means it is gone from most of its former territory and now exists only in a few places.

ENDANGERED

Burrowing owl

Burrowing owls have been poisoned by farm insecticides and rodent poisons and shot by farmers who mistake them for gophers. Their nesting sites in prairie fields have been filled in by tractors. The burrowing owl is listed as threatened because, unless things change, it will become endangered. Cooperation from farmers can give the burrowing owls a chance to recover.

The North Pacific humpback whale, the Great Lakes deepwater sculpin and the Kentucky coffee tree are also threatened species.

THREATENED

VULNERABLE

Eastern bluebird

Swallows and house wrens chase Eastern bluebirds from their nesting sites; cities and farms reduce their habitat; storms, parasites and pesticides take their toll. No wonder the Eastern bluebird is listed as vulnerable. Fortunately, concerned birdwatchers noticed the bluebird's decline and got to work building nesting boxes so bluebirds could raise their young in safety. It is hoped that this will stop the species from becoming threatened and then endangered.

Other vulnerable species include the Pacific sardine, the prairie rose and the spotted bat.

DELISTED

White pelican

This big-billed fishing bird was once listed as endangered. Its numbers had fallen because its nesting grounds were disturbed by people and its food was poisoned with chemicals. People became worried. They passed laws to ban one of the main chemical poisons, DDT, and to protect the white pelican's nesting sites. Today the pelicans are healthy and off the endangered species list!

15

EXTINCTION IS FOREVER

You reach down and pick up a chunk of rock. When you flip it over, you're surprised to see that you've got a trilobite fossil in your hand. It's the only remains of a tiny sea creature that lived more than 400 million years ago.

Trilobites are long extinct. So are dinosaurs, saber-toothed tigers and millions of other plants and animals that have lived on the earth and then vanished forever. There are few clues to tell us why they became extinct. Most died off slowly. Over millions of years, they became vulnerable, then endangered, then extinct. When these natural extinctions happened, other species evolved to fill their places or whole new species took over from the old ones.

But today a new kind of extinction is changing the world. It's a speeded-up extinction that happens so fast new creatures can't evolve quickly enough to fill all the vacancies. Try eating some raisins to see what happens when extinction accelerates. You'll need two lunch-sized boxes of raisins. Eat the first box of raisins one at a time. Record on a piece of paper the number of swallows it takes to finish the raisins. Now eat the second box of raisins at a two times accelerated rate. Start by eating one raisin. The next mouthful, eat two times the last mouthful. Keep doubling with each mouthful. So that's 1 raisin, then 2, then 2 x 2, then 4 x 2 and so on. Keep doubling until you've made all the raisins "extinct." Record the number of swallows and compare.

The first box of raisins is a natural extinction, the second is an accelerated extinction. Tasty mathematics, but imagine if the raisins were animals.

Today, one species becomes extinct every 15 minutes. Sometimes humans hunt animals to extinction for food or for blubber, ivory and other valuable body parts. But other times the damage is accidental. Humans destroy many animal habitats to make room for cities or farms. We also spray crops with fertilizers and pesticides and accidentally poison the animals who eat them.

Fortunately, wildlife is tough. A species can recover from the brink of extinction — with help from humans. Yes, humans can help as well as harm wildlife. For some ideas on how you can turn human harm into human help, turn to pages 82 – 85.

ildlife close-up: The mastodon

Add fur to an African elephant and you'd have an animal that resembles a mastodon. But you won't see any mastodons around today; they've been extinct for 6000 years.

Mastodons lived on earth for millions of years. During that time, huge ice sheets swept across the northern hemisphere and then retreated again when the land warmed. Mastodons adjusted their bodies and eating habits in small ways and were able to survive these climate changes.

But as the land grew warmer and drier at the end of the last ice age, the lush swampy evergreen forests that mastodons depended on for food began to thin out. This time, mastodons didn't adjust and their numbers slowly fell. Moose and woodland caribou moved into the new sparse forest swamps and took the place of the mastodon. The mastodon disappeared from the earth in a natural extinction.

ildlife close-up: The great auk

The great auk looked a lot like a penguin. It was a flightless black-and-white seabird that dove for fish in the north Atlantic Ocean. Once a year, tens of millions of great auks gathered on rocky islands and nested in huge, squawking colonies.

Around 1500, European fishermen started slaughtering the birds and collecting their eggs. The adults stood guard at their nests even as the hunters swung their clubs. In 1760, European feather collectors joined the hunt. They attacked the breeding colonies and boiled the feathers off all the auks they killed.

On June 3, 1844, three fishermen near Iceland found the last breeding pair of great auks and their egg. They killed the adults, and one of the fishermen, Ketil Ketilsson, smashed the last egg with his boot. In 350 short years, the number of great auks went from tens of millions to zero. That's accelerated extinction.

17

ENDANGERED SPECIES

Suppose you could slip into a wild animal costume and spend a year living in the wild. No more piano lessons or homework or chores! You'd be free to wander anywhere you pleased. Or would you?

Being a wild animal is dangerous these days. Hunters track you, water holes are poisoned with chemicals, and your home may be gobbled up by a growing city. Everywhere you turn, danger lurks.

You can help threatened animals and plants. The first step: understanding. Read on for more info on the hazards facing wildlife. The next step: take action. Find out what other kids have done to help and how you can join in.

DON'T SHOOT

Ever dreamed you're whale watching on the open seas? The captain gives you the telescope, barking, "Watch to starboard." Suddenly, a hulking grey island heaves out of the depths, only a stone's throw from the boat. A hot, wet spray of breath mists over your raincoat. The shiny island is changing shape. There's a tail. You holler "Captain, there's a right whale." But the captain raises his harpoon gun and takes aim. This is a nightmare.

In real life, you'd be extremely lucky to see a northern right whale. There are only about 300 left in the world. They have been hunted to near extinction. Despite a 50-year-old ban on hunting, there may be too few of them, spread over too great a distance, to bring the population back to a healthy number. Right whales may become extinct before the year 2000.

Right whales got their name because they were the right ones to shoot. Why? They feed on plankton and krill near the surface. As they feed, the whales swim very slowly and seldom dive, so they are easy for hunters to locate. They are not afraid of boats or people, and at 60 feet (18 m) long, they are big targets. Unlike their large relatives the blue and grey whales, right whales float when harpooned, making them easy to haul on board.

The right whales were hunted for their baleen and blubber. Right whales have baleen instead of teeth. To eat, they gulp in huge quantities of seawater, then squirt it back out, catching krill and plankton on their baleen.

Baleen was precious in the days before steel because it was strong but bendable. It was used to make such things as umbrellas and corsets. One whale could yield up to one ton of baleen — that's a lot of umbrellas.

The Right Stuff

Scientists are trying to help the right whale make a comeback. To do this, they need to know how the whale lives, what it eats and where it travels.

Scientists at Guelph University in Ontario study the right whale in the Bay of Fundy off Nova Scotia. Using a modified crossbow, they shoot a dart equipped with a radio transmitter into a whale. (The dart doesn't cause pain, though it can irritate the skin of the whale.) By monitoring signals the transmitter beeps back, they learn about depth of feeding, location, socializing and much more. The Guelph team has found that the right whales of the St. Lawrence River prefer to travel on the main shipping routes. This helps explain why so many young whales are killed by ships.

When the whales move south, they are studied by scientists from the University of Maine. Right whales have rough warty patches, called callosities, on their heads, throats and bellies. Photographs and underwater videos are taken to identify individual whales by these distinctive skin markings. Together the Canadian and U.S. teams are gaining more information on this endangered species.

Whales' blubber was also valuable. When melted down into oil, it was used to fuel lamps. Right whales have a layer of blubber as thick as 24 inches (60 cm).

Commercial whaling began with the right whale and then spread to the other giant whales. Today the southern right, bowhead, humpback and blue whales are all "commercially extinct." This means there are too few of them to make a profitable harvest for whalers. The whaling industry was very shortsighted. Whalers put themselves out of jobs by nearly wiping whales off the map.

R.I.P.

The following species have been hunted to extinction:

Carolina parakeet
Elephant bird
Himalayan Mountain quail
Pink-headed duck
Newfoundland white wolf
Texas grey wolf
Mexican silver grizzly bear
Bali tiger
Arizona jaguar
Blue buck
Dawson's caribou
Steller's sea cow
Sea mink
Caribbean monk seal

SPOT THE WILDLIFE PRODUCTS

This family is really thoughtless. They have adorned themselves and their home with endangered wildlife products. Even their pets are rare and exotic. Can you spot all 20 wild things? See page 96 for the answers.

BLOW THE HORN ON WILDLIFE TRADE

Why would anyone want a pair of snakeskin cowboy boots if they knew an endangered snake was killed to make them? Maybe because of fashion, or because they meant something special to the wearer. Even though laws now protect many endangered animals, hunters still kill them and illegally sell fashionable or special body parts to eager buyers.

 ildlife close-up: The elephant

Since 1981, the number of elephants left in the wild has been cut in half. Three hundred are killed every day. Several are destroyed by angry farmers whose crops are trampled by browsing herds. A few are hunted for sport. But most are shot for their tusks. African elephant tusks are ivory, which is used in carvings, piano keys, even billiard balls.

Ivory has been called "white gold." The value of two tusks is equal to what the average African earns in one year. Governments try to limit the number of elephants killed and use some of the money from ivory sales to pay for conservation projects. But the temptation to kill elephants illegally is great. The only solution seems to be to stop the sale of all ivory.

Like people, elephants are social creatures. They live in large, close, family groups. The death of an elephant affects the entire family. If a mother is killed, the young perish. The older, large-tusked males take with them unborn offspring.

The killing of elephants also affects other wildlife. Elephants are giant seed-dispersal machines; they eat plants and disperse the seeds in their excrement. If they become extinct, plants that depend on them will be threatened, too.

Is it too late to save the elephants? Pessimists say they will be extinct in the wild by 2030. Maybe. Then again, maybe not. People can help stop the slaughter by refusing to buy ivory. Consumers have power. People's anger over the disappearance of the whales and big spotted cats has nearly stopped trade in whale products and coats made from big cat fur.

Traditions are important but attitudes can be changed. A poacher can earn money as a tourist guide, and it's legal. With luck, conservation and wildlife management, we can save the elephant from becoming a memory.

Wildlife close-up: The rhinoceros

Pity the poor rhinoceros. Rhino horn is used in Yemen to make dagger handles that are given to boys at the age they become men. Even though all five kinds of rhinos are classified as endangered and protected by law, poachers (illegal hunters) shoot them for their horns. Plastic dagger handles won't do and it's the rhino who pays — with its life.

A recent drastic experiment involved trapping and drugging rhinos, sawing off and destroying their horns, and then releasing the beasts again into the wild. This foiled poachers, but proved disastrous for the rhino. Without his horn, a male rhino can't find a mate. He becomes an outcast.

Kids Make Headlines

Student members of World Wildlife Fund in Switzerland took to the streets to protest the ivory trade. Waving banners and wearing sweatshirts with a big tusked elephant on the front, they shouted out their demands: Stop the trade of all ivory now, forever! They got international press coverage, which spread their message worldwide.

FOOD POISONING

Suppose you're baby-sitting and the four-year-old cuts his knee just before bed. To get his mind off it, you give him a bandage and a nice big glass of juice. Then you find a note from the parents asking you not to give him anything to drink before bed — bedwetting problems. Oh-oh...you solved one problem but caused another.

Although a wet bed in the middle of the night is unpleasant, it's hardly a disaster. But when good intentions go wrong in nature, the results can be tragic. For example, when farmers and foresters spray pesticides to kill the insects that eat their crops, they can accidentally poison birds and mammals, too.

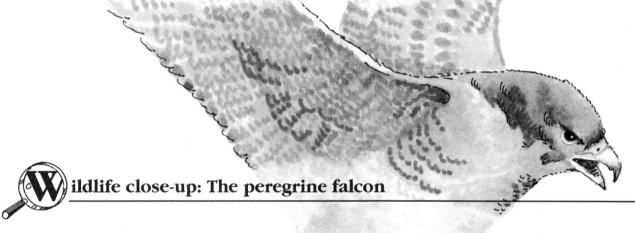

Wildlife close-up: The peregrine falcon

A peregrine falcon roosts on a rocky crag scanning the valley below for a tasty lunch. In the distance, it spies a fat golden plover flying along a riverbank. The chase is on. In a few swift beats of its long wings, the peregrine is directly over the plover. It flings itself downwards in a hurtling wedge of beak and claw. The plover is struck at 185 miles (300 km) an hour and tumbles dead to the ground.

The peregrine lands beside its prey and feasts on the warm flesh and blood. Sadly, the well-earned meal is causing the extinction of the peregrine. Last year, all the eggs broke in its nest before they were ready to hatch. This year they will too.

It took scientists a long time to figure out that peregrine falcon young die — sometimes before they hatch — because of the food their parents eat.

The plover, like many of the birds the peregrine falcon eats, is contaminated with chemicals. How did this happen?

Each winter, plovers leave northern Canada and migrate to the plains of Argentina. There they eat insects and grubs that have been sprayed with pesticides. On their way north in the spring, the plovers stop to feed in American grainfields, again on grubs and insects that have been sprayed. All these meals, spiced with small amounts of pesticide, don't affect the plovers much, but the poisons pass on from insect to plover to falcon. Each meal adds another dose to the falcon's body. Scientists say the pesticides travel up the falcon's food chain.

The slow collection of poisons in the peregrine doesn't hurt the adult bird. But when the mother starts to lay her eggs, they are soft-shelled and deformed. It's easy for the adult birds to accidentally crush these soft-shelled eggs. The result: very few young hatch alive.

World Wildlife Fund and other organizations are trying to help the peregrine falcon. They have called for a worldwide ban on dangerous pesticides such as DDT. So far, Canada and the U.S. have agreed to the ban. Unfortunately, several countries in Central and South America still use the pesticides.

Ospreys and bald eagles are also threatened by pesticide use. When DDT is sprayed on fields and forests to kill mosquitoes, rain may flush the left-over chemicals into lakes and rivers. Eventually the poisons find their way into the bodies of fish. Ospreys and bald eagles are big fish eaters, and slowly the pesticides collect in their bodies. Once again, it's the broken eggshells that tell the story.

Chain Reaction

This game is similar to Battleship, only instead of finding ships, you're going to be a peregrine falcon in search of birds to eat. But beware: some of the birds you find may have eaten poisonous pesticides. Eat them and you'll be in trouble, too.

You'll need:
2 sheets of graph paper
a pencil
a red pen
a ruler
a clock

Setting up:
You and a friend each take a sheet of graph paper and separate from one another to prepare. No peeking! Each player follows these instructions:

1. Divide one sheet of graph paper in half. On the top half, pencil off a square 10 lines across and 10 lines down with a ruler. Do the same thing on the bottom half. On both squares label the lines across the top "1" to "10" and the lines down the side "a" to "j." Name the top set of squares "My Territory" and the bottom square "Opponent's Territory."

2. On your Opponent's Territory draw 10 birds, some covering three intersections (places where two lines cross), some covering four. Color four birds (two of each size) red. Your opponent will have to find these birds as the game is played. And you will have to find the birds your opponent has drawn on her territory. It's time for both of you to become peregrine falcons and find your prey.

3. Sit across a table from your friend and put a mountain range of books between you so you can't see each other's graph paper. One of you starts by calling coordinates (for example, c-3, or a-7), trying to find the birds hidden from you. When you get lucky and find part of a bird, call nearby coordinates and try to find

the whole bird. Record your moves on the graph paper called My Territory. Sometimes you may find part of a bird but then call a wrong coordinate and miss the rest of the bird. When this happens, you lose your turn and your friend takes a turn. See how many birds each of you can "catch" in 15 minutes.

4. Score 2 points for every small bird you've caught and 3 points for every big bird. But beware! If you've caught too many birds that have been contaminated with pesticides (the ones colored red), you're in trouble. Count up the pesticide-free birds (those *not* colored red) and see how you've done.
• A healthy peregrine population must have 10 clean points.
• An endangered peregrine population has 7-9 clean points.
• An extinct peregrine population has under 7 clean points. Ask yourself, did pesticide-contaminated food, or lack of food, cause the extinction?

Pesticide Patrol

Guard against careless pesticide use and disposal around your home. Instead of using chemical pesticides, plant onions, marigolds and garlic to keep insect pests away from your garden. Or use friendly insects to control insect pests. Your local nursery can identify species, such as the ladybug, that destroy pests naturally. Ordinary soap and water, sprayed on plants, discourages insect pests, too.

Don't throw old cans of pesticide out in the garbage. The pesticides can leak out and into nearby water, poisoning fish and the birds that eat them. Phone the public works department in your city or town to find where it's safe to dispose of toxic waste such as pesticides, old batteries and paint.

BAD NEWS NUMBERS

Imagine a game of tag with only two players. It wouldn't be fair or fun. Most games have a "right" number of players. Go below that number and the game won't work. A scientist might call the lowest number of players the "sustainable number" for the game. With fewer numbers, the game can't be played, or "sustained."

Animal species have sustainable numbers too. This is the number of animals needed to keep the species going. There must be enough animals to find mates and have young. After all, without young, the species won't survive.

When a species begins to decline in numbers, it's sometimes hard to put on the brakes and stop. Chances are, the animal will skid below its sustainable number and into extinction.

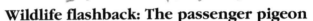

Wildlife flashback: The passenger pigeon
Fifty years before the last passenger pigeon died, no one would have believed the population could ever fall below its sustainable number.

- 1813, Louisville, Kentucky — The passenger pigeon is named the most numerous bird on earth. J.J. Audubon, the noted ornithologist, estimates that billions fly up the Ohio River valley. One expert calculates a billion birds eat a million bushels of food a day.

- 1850, Manistee River, Michigan — Chief Pokagon hears a distant rumbling. He fears a huge army is advancing on his tribe and sets out to investigate. It turns out to be millions of passenger pigeons flying in to nest in nearby woods. He reports that the weight of so many birds and nests actually breaks mature trees, and the birds' dung covers the forest floor like snow. Hundreds of thousands of fat squabs (young pigeons) are successfully raised and the parent birds move on to nest again.

- 1870, Cincinnati, Ohio — The noonday sun is blackened by birds. An expert counts 2 billion birds in one flock. Another flock measures 320 miles (515 km) long and 1 mile (1.6 km) wide.

• 1878, Petoskey, Michigan — To satisfy the market for pigeon and squab meat, pigeon hunters kill a billion birds at a single nesting site. The hunters use "stool pigeons," fluttering birds with eyes sewn shut and feet tied to stools, to lure the victims into their killing nets. Birds are sold by the boxcar load in New York for food, feathers and medicine.

• 1896, Bowling Green, Ohio — Hunters attack the last large flock of pigeons, numbering 250,000 adults. The hunters kill 200,000 of the adults, mutilate more than 40,000 others and destroy 100,000 chicks. Ten thousand birds get away.

The dead birds are shipped to New York, but the train derails. All the pigeon carcasses rot and have to be dumped.

• 1900, Pike County, Ohio — A boy shoots the last wild passenger pigeon.

• 1914, Cincinnati Zoo, Ohio — The last captive passenger pigeon, Martha, dies at age 29.

The impossible happened. From billions of birds, the species became extinct in less than 50 years. The population was hunted below its sustainable number and could not recover.

Going, going, gone

The passenger pigeon isn't alone. In the last 200 years, hundreds of other wildlife species have been hunted, poisoned, poached, driven from their homes and otherwise hounded below their sustainable numbers and are now extinct.

Today, some living species are doomed to extinction because people have pushed their numbers too low. The California condor is one. There are so few condors left that they may never mate in the wild again.

The wild African violet is another. Only three of these plants are known to be left in the world.

Other species that have been pushed below their sustainable numbers include: bumblebee bat, pygmy hog, Mediterranean monk seal, angonoka (Madagascar land tortoise), woolly spider monkey, Queen Alexandra's Birdwing butterfly, golden toad and Eskimo curlew. The animals you read about in the preceding pages — right whale, rhinoceros and peregrine falcon — may soon fall below their sustainable numbers, too.

BALANCING THE NUMBERS

Sit on a teeter-totter opposite a friend and what happens? At first, one person crashes to the ground while the other ends up stranded high in the air. To get the teeter totter balancing properly, you both have to make adjustments.

The same kind of thing happens to wildlife populations. A population explosion in one species throws nature off balance. But gradually the population is brought back into balance. Either predators step in and reduce the number, or the growing population can't find enough food or shelter and starts to shrink again. These adjustments soon bring the population into balance.

Without human interference, the natural world performs a graceful balancing act. As long as a species' numbers are sustainable, the population will stay a healthy size. Humans can upset nature's delicate balance. Even wildlife scientists who are sensitive to the dangers of human interference can accidentally mess things up. So they have to be very careful when they're trying to help a wildlife population.

 Wildlife close-up: The tundra, the caribou and the wolf

Barren ground caribou travel in herds that can number tens of thousands. They search for their favorite food, the lichens that grow on rocky, tundra soil.

Packs of wolves travel alongside the caribou herd. Their leader waits until one caribou strays from the group and then launches an attack. Some hunters say that killing off wolves would let caribou populations grow much bigger. But would it?

It's not just the hungry wolves that determine the size of the caribou population. It's also the availability of food, water, living space, shelter and other things the caribou need to survive.

One wolf eats 20 to 25 small caribou a year. In places where all the wolves are killed, the caribou flourish — for a while. But then there are too many caribou for the food supply, and some starve. The wolves actually help to make sure that this doesn't happen. When humans interfere and kill the wolves, more wildlife ends up dead than if the natural balances are left alone.

Wildlife close-up: The tundra, the lemming and the snowy owl

Lemmings, or Arctic "mice," breed rapidly for several years until there is a population explosion. Soon their food supply is exhausted and there's a dramatic population crash. Few of the young survive. If they do, they start migrating in huge numbers and sometimes run over high cliffs or into the sea, killing themselves. No one knows for certain why this happens.

Meanwhile, the snowy owls that eat the lemmings have been growing in number, too.

When the lemming population falls, the owls fly hundreds of miles (kilometers) south in a desperate search for food. About every four years, bird-watchers in southern Canada and the northern United States find these hungry refugee owls hunting around airports or flat country that looks like their home in the north.

Back on the Arctic tundra, a small number of the lemmings and snowy owls look for mates and start the cycle again.

The Wild Side

Encourage wildlife to take over part of your backyard. Build a simple bird feeder and keep it stocked up with seed all winter long. Change to a hummingbird feeder in summer and keep it filled with tasty syrup. Build or buy a bird house or a bat box (you can find instructions for making them at your local library) and then listen in spring for the squeaks of the young you've sheltered.

WILDLIFE CLOSE-UP: THE WHOOPING CRANE

All eyes are on the whooping crane, a bird that's fighting its way back from near extinction. Binoculars, cameras, special tracking equipment and just plain eyeballs desperately try to spot, follow, count and study the few whoopers that remain on earth. Millions of hours and millions of dollars have been spent to save the whooper from disappearing. No wonder the whooping crane is the symbol of endangered species all over North America.

Why is the whooper in trouble? The whooping crane population was probably never more than 1500, spread over a large range. Then people began to settle in western Canada and drain the marshlands where whoopers had nested and raised their young for thousands of years. The vast prairie was cut up into ranches and towns. Railways and roads criss-crossed the wilderness where migrating cranes had always stopped to feed. The whoopers' territory shrank and their numbers fell quickly.

Egg collecting, a hobby popular in the last century, added to the whoopers' problems. Museums and individuals competed for eggs. Unborn whoopers, vital to the species' survival, were entombed in display cases.

Hunters shot the whooper for food and trophies. They were an easy target because they are large and always travel the same routes. The killing continued despite growing concern for the whooper's survival. In 1916, whooping cranes were protected by law, but whoopers continued to be shot, often in error when hunters mistook them for other large game birds. Six birds out of a tiny flock of about 21 were gunned down during migration in the early 1950s.

Today all the whoopers in the world fly on a single migration route, instead of several. They nest each summer within the boundaries of Wood Buffalo National Park in Canada's north and winter in 30 square miles (80 square kilometers) in the Aransas Wildlife Refuge in Texas. They live so close together that one catastrophe could eliminate them all. It's happened before. In the 1950s, an entire flock of whoopers, living in Louisiana, perished in a hurricane.

Migration Is Not a Vacation

In late autumn, the whoopers leave their summer home in the Wood Buffalo National Park in the Northwest Territories for their winter home in the Aransas Wildlife Refuge in Texas, 2175 miles (3500 km) away. They rest and eat grains in the fields of Saskatchewan for up to two weeks. If they stay too long, an early snowstorm may take them by surprise.

The whoopers fly over big cities and open farmland for nine to 13 days, sharing the sky with airplanes, high tension wires and pollution from the midwest. When the whoopers touch down to feed in Nebraska or Kansas, biologists "babysit" them. They can't be too careful because it's hunting season, and sometimes a whooper is mistaken for a lesser snow goose, a white pelican or a sandhill crane. What do you think the chances are of making the trip successfully?

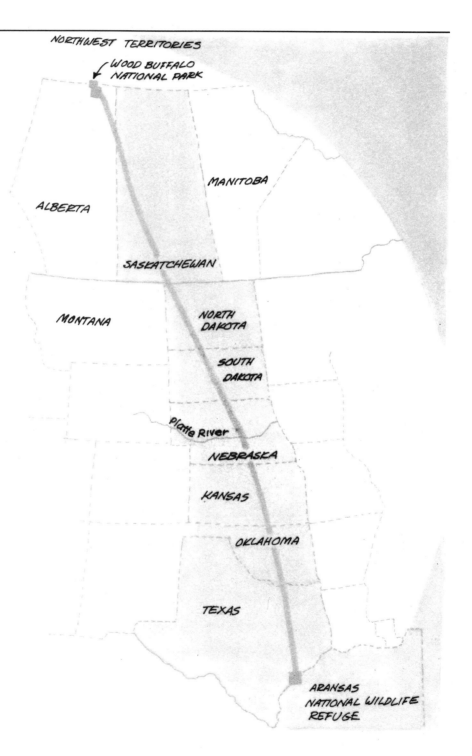

Coins for Cranes

Whooping crane eggs are about 4 inches (10 cm) long and 2 ½ inches (6 cm) high — about the size of an avocado. They can be light brown or buffy olive with dark brown and purplish blotches. The large end is often a solid brown. This coloring helps to camouflage the egg in its nest of bulrushes and sedge grass. The eggs are smooth and glossy.

Here's how to make an "eggciting" money bank that is the size and color of a whooping crane egg. Before you start, spread your working area with newspaper. Papier mâché is fun but messy!

You'll need:

a small balloon
newspaper, cut in strips 1 inch x 6 inches (3 cm x 15 cm)
flour and water paste
a knife or scissors
water-based paints
a paint brush
shellac (optional)
a cork

1. Blow up your balloon to slightly smaller than the desired size and tie it tightly.

2. Dip the newspaper strips in the paste and cover the balloon with a single layer of strips, leaving a hole the size of a cork where the balloon is tied.

3. Let it dry. Apply several layers of strips in this fashion building up the size and shape of the egg. This project may take a few days, but not nearly as long as the 29 to 30 days it takes a parent whooper to incubate an egg.

4. With an adult supervising, cut a hole big enough for a large coin in the top of the egg. Pop and pull out the balloon.

5. Let the egg dry thoroughly.

6. Paint. Dry again. Shellac and dry again. Now insert your cork.

Share your eggcitement! Take your creation to school and show it to your class. Save your coins. When your egg is full, send its contents to World Wildlife Fund or a local conservation group, to help wildlife.

Kids Help Protect Platte River Staging Area

In 1980, a magazine article alerted North American kids that the Platte River in Nebraska was a critical habitat for migrating whoopers as well as their sandhill crane cousins. Pennies, nickels and dimes poured into the National Audubon Society with the plea, "Please save the cranes' feeding grounds." A concrete bunker was built so people can watch and photograph the birds without disturbing them. This bunker, or blind, is dedicated to the kids of North America.

JET SET EGGS

The United States and Canada are working together on a rescue mission.

Earlier this century, both countries passed laws protecting whooping cranes. Hunting was made illegal and the whoopers' remaining habitat was protected. Canadian nesting sites and American wintering grounds were both declared national parks. The two countries agreed to guard the migration corridor. Still, the whooper population failed to recover.

Thirty years ago, scientists decided to get involved. Step one was to learn everything possible about the whooper. Little details about behavior and habitat might give clues to the birds' needs. Maybe then the slide to extinction could be halted.

Studies of whooper eggs gave scientists a start. Whoopers lay two eggs, but raise only one chick. What would happen if scientists stole the "spare" egg and tried to raise a whooper in captivity?

A whooper orphanage was set up in Maryland, where the spare eggs were hatched and the chicks

raised without parents. The scheme worked beautifully. The eggs left in the wild hatched and so did the orphan eggs. But the captive (orphan) birds failed to breed. In 1975, equipped with all they had learned, scientists decided to take the project one step further. Some of the "stolen" eggs were taken by aircraft from Wood Buffalo National Park to Gray's Lake National Wildlife Refuge in Idaho. Here they were placed in the nests of the greater sandhill crane, a cousin of the whooping crane. The sandhill cranes were going to be foster parents and raise the young whoopers.

The foster parents seemed to accept the eggs if the egg's placement in the new nest was done carefully. Timing was critical. Unhatched whooper chicks start to tap on the inside of the egg a few days before hatching. The tapping is thought to be the first communication between the chick and its parents, signaling to the parent: "Hey, I'm in here, about to hatch. What's for lunch?" The parents answer back with squawks and nuzzles, "We're here, ready and waiting. Hope you like frogs." If an egg was already tapping when put into a sandhill foster parent's nest, the sandhills became suspicious and rolled the egg out. So the eggs had to be transferred before the tapping started.

For five years, the experiment seemed to be working. Lots of chicks hatched and they were healthy. Sadly, as time went on, it became obvious that the "fostered birds" were not normal. They knew they weren't sandhill cranes, but they didn't know they were whoopers. During migration, they became confused; males flew one way, females another. Whooping crane "radar" is usually excellent. But the radar of these fostered whoopers had gone haywire.

In July 1989, the program was stopped. The 12 surviving fostered birds remain a mysterious puzzle and will never have young whoopers.

So it is back to the drawing board for the scientists. The failed foster program told them what didn't work. Now the question is, what *will* work?

The U.S.-Canada team has set two difficult goals: to have a total of 200 whooping cranes by the year 2000 and to start a separate breeding colony with the captive population by the year 2010. In the meantime, government experts and planes will swoop in to rescue sick or injured birds at a moment's notice. And scientists keep looking for any other ways to help. Canada and the U.S. are determined not to let the whooper down.

MR. WHOOPING CRANE

It is a frosty dawn in Wood Buffalo National Park. The male whooping crane flaps his fully spread wings over his head, while his long neck yo-yos up and down. Loud bugle-like whoops break the silence of the northern morning. The calls can be heard more than half a mile (one kilometer) away. The whooper is claiming his mate and his territory.

A month later, an alarm clock goes off in an Edmonton bedroom. It is time for Ernie Kuyt, a Canadian Wildlife Service biologist, to go in search of the cranes. He scrambles into his clothes and heads for the airfield.

Each spring Ernie Kuyt follows the same routine. From his rented plane, Ernie swoops over the pairs of whoopers and adds a check to his list. They're back, too! After six sweeps over the park, he has located and counted all the nesting pairs. It's a good year — most of the birds arrived safely from their winter homes in Texas.

The whoopers ignore the plane high above them. They are busy nest-building. Scratching the snow, they find last year's hollow-stemmed bulrushes, their favorite nesting material. They choose a nesting site out in the marsh, to make it harder for egg-snatching foxes and coyotes to get to them. The nest sits above the waterline, like a large chair cushion, fenced in with rushes and weeds. No wonder it's difficult to spot — the nest and swamp blend together.

The hum of the aircraft turns to a roar. Here comes Ernie again. This time he's flying low over the nest, sending the parents running and squawking with alarm. A quick pass with the binoculars tells him there are two eggs on the nest. Now it's back home to plan his next visit to the cranes.

The parent whoopers listen to the plane's roar fade away and cautiously return to the eggs. Taking turns, they sit on the nest and feed in a nearby shallow lake. A rustling in the bulrushes alerts the female that a coyote is dangerously close. The male returns quickly, and with a fierce display of wings and beak, sends the intruder loping away, without breakfast.

Ernie checks his equipment. Yes, there are his maps, notes and plenty of woolly socks. It's egg-snatching time and the helicopter is waiting. Ernie and the pilot are a pair of pros. The pilot lands the helicopter as close to the nest as possible, frightening the parents away. Ernie jumps out, wearing his wading boots. In his hands are two trusty sticks used for balance, judging the depth of the water and measuring the nest and eggs. He thrashes his way to the nest and scoops up one egg. He quickly plops it into the cold swamp water. It floats and makes tiny wiggles and waves, telling him that inside there's a live chick. He repeats this with the second egg. Both are alive. Now there is a chance for two whoopers to live instead of just one. Eeny-meeny, it doesn't really matter now. Drying them carefully, he slips one back into the nest and slides the other into a sock he carries with him.

Then it's back to the helicopter and off to the next nest. The engine whines with take-off and the parents return to their remaining egg. It's been just three minutes since the human intruder scared them away.

Within hours, the single egg in the nest taps and the parents reply with low, growling noises. After 29 days of sitting and waiting, the parents are rewarded with the hatching of a reddish-orange chick. Just one day later, the young whooper is ready to walk about the marsh, exploring and feeding with its watchful parents.

The egg in the sock spends the night at Ernie Kuyt's home. It and other stolen eggs are kept in a portable incubator heated with hot water bottles. The next day, the eggs are packed as carefully as precious crystal and airlifted to Maryland, where they will hatch and be kept in captivity. Ernie's spring job is over; he takes a well-deserved summer holiday.

Egg snatching gives both chicks a better chance. The wild chick gets its parents' full attention, so it has a better chance of surviving. The other egg would have perished in the wild. In captivity, it provides scientists with a wealth of information about the whooping cranes. It is like a bird in a bank — savings for the future.

Ernie Kuyt makes one last visit to the wild whooper families in August. He must collar-band the young before they are good flyers. These collar-bands look like wide dog's collars and identify each new bird, making them easy to spot and count.

After testing their wings with short hops between marshes, the young whoopers leave for their first migration at the end of September. They follow their parents on the 2175 mile (3500 km) flight to the wintering grounds in Texas.

Ernie Kuyt watches the cranes flying south. Next year he will return to check on them. And to steal more eggs for the captive colony he and other scientists are trying to build. With luck, one day this captive colony may become a second whooping crane population living in the wild. Thanks to the efforts of Mr. Whooping Crane (Ernie Kuyt) and other concerned scientists, there are now 150 whoopers living in the wild and the 60 held in captivity in Maryland. The whooper is making a comeback.

41

SUCCESS STORIES

Sure there are lots of sad stories about wildlife, but there are successes, too. People have identified species that are near extinction and have found ways to help them. With care and a bit of luck, a number of once-endangered animals are now able to make a go of survival.

The muskox in Canada

A hundred years ago, people wanted muskox rugs in their sleighs, so hunters went out and shot the animals. Muskoxen are easy marks for hunters because when danger approaches, the slow-moving adults form a defensive ring around their young. This circling works well against wolves, but it only makes it easier for people to shoot whole herds at a time.

In 1917, the Canadian government outlawed all muskox hunting. By 1990, the muskox had recovered from a low of 2000 to a population of 50 000 in northern Canada. Now that's a success story!

The tiger in India

India was once home to 40 000 tigers. A very few of them, the old and the sick, became man-eaters. Villagers who killed those tigers were local heroes. Unfortunately, healthy tigers, not known to be man-eaters, were hunted too. By the late 1800s, tiger hunting became the ultimate trophy sport. In 1972, the number of tigers in India fell below 2000.

In 1973, Operation Tiger was launched by the Government of India and World Wildlife Fund. Nine reserves were set aside for the big cats to prowl in, safely. When people-tiger confrontations occur in the reserves, special squads remove the problem tigers to zoos or other, wilder reserves. Real man-eaters are eliminated. In Sundarbans, where tigers have harassed fishermen, woodcutters and honey collectors for centuries, the squads set out to teach them a lesson. Using electrically wired human dummies, the squads arranged for meddling tigers to give themselves a nasty shock. Those tigers stay away from people now.

After 12 years of Operation Tiger, the number of tigers in India has increased to 4000.

The sea otter of the Pacific coast

In the 1800s, sea otters were slaughtered for their fur throughout the north Pacific Ocean until only a few remained off California and Alaska. No sea otters were left in Canada. In 1911, Russia, Canada, the U.S. and Japan banned the hunt.

Fortunately, sea otters in Alaska and the Aleutian Islands recovered on their own. The southern sea otters off California recovered somewhat, but remain threatened by fishermen who kill them, thinking the otters eat too many shellfish.

In Canada between 1969 and 1972, scientists introduced 89 Alaskan otters to a sheltered stretch of Vancouver Island shoreline. Today that number has grown to about 350. But the sea otter is still considered endangered in Canada. One bad oil spill could wipe out all the otters. Oil spilled from the oil tanker *Exxon Valdez* in Alaska killed more than 1000. If Canadian sea otter numbers increase and if the colonies spread over a wider length of coastline, scientists predict the survival of the species in Canada will be assured.

ENDANGERED SPACES

Do you have a favorite wild place? Maybe a campsite or a park or even an abandoned lot that's gone wild? Next time you visit it, check out all the plants and animals that live there. Animals need wilderness habitats (homes) where they can find food, water, shelter and a safe place to raise their young.

What would happen if your wild place were surrounded by houses or bulldozed to make room for a highway? What if it were polluted with chemicals or trash? Your little patch of wilderness would be endangered — and so would the plants and animals who live in it.

Read on to find out why habitats are in trouble — and what you can do to help.

WILDERNESS — WHO NEEDS IT?

The baked beans are rumbling their way through your stomach, as you lick the marshmallow off your lips. The fire's last embers glow red, and night descends around your camp site. Looking up through the tall conifers, you see the first twinkling stars. Crickets chorus nearby and coyotes yip in the distance. Take cover, here comes a low-flying bat! Wilderness is a pleasure that gives us a break from the usual routine. For wildlife, wilderness is home. If wilderness is plowed under for farms and cities, polluted with chemicals, chopped down or even converted into a ski resort, the animals and plants living there will suffer. Destruction of their habitat (wildlife homes) is the main reason plants and animals become endangered.

Animals need wilderness to survive. How much wilderness? One way to find out is to watch the carnivores (meat eaters). Bears, wolverines, bobcats and other carnivores need a big habitat in order to find enough food. If the number of carnivores falls, it means there isn't enough food. And this means the carnivores' prey are in trouble, too. So carnivores tell us something about the health of the habitat.

Get Your Mind Into Wilderness

Next time you curl up in your sleeping bag, try this wilderness listening activity.

Get comfortable. Shut your eyes. Listen to the noises in the woods around you. It's not peaceful and quiet but loud with life. Tune in closer — blocking out the distant waterfall or coyote. Do you hear an owl? Crickets? Raccoons?

Now zero in on the camp site. Is the wet wood on the fire spitting? Is a squirrel scratching for leftovers?

Zoom in even closer. Is your watch ticking? Is a mosquito buzzing in your ear? Is your sleeping bag rubbing on the grass?

Try ignoring all other sounds and listen to yourself. Breathe in and out, slowly and steadily. Feel your skin tingle, your toenails grow. Now focus on your heartbeat. Thump, thump.

P.S. You can try this in the city, too. You won't hear many wild animals but you may find that by concentrating on certain noises, such as a bird in the garden, you can block out the city sounds.

The wolverine's name means "glutton" or "great eater" in Swedish. To satisfy its greedy appetite, the wolverine needs large areas of wilderness where prey is plentiful. Wolverines keep competitors out by defending their home with a fierceness that has earned them the nickname "devil beast."

There have never been lots of wolverines, but hunting, trapping and poisoning have made them even rarer. Now their remaining habitat is shrinking. Unlike grizzlies, most wolverines don't want anything to do with people — they even turn their noses up at garbage.

Wildlife close-up: The grizzly bear

Tens of thousands of grizzlies used to range through the middle of North America, but then the pioneers moved in. A growing population of people gradually forced the grizzlies into a narrow strip of land on the west coast.

Grizzlies are loners and need an enormous territory — from 10 000 to 16 500 square miles (26 000 to 43 000 square kilometers). They wander throughout their territory searching for food. In spring, they eat emerging plants such as the tender shoots of avalanche lilies that grow on alpine slopes. They fish for salmon and hunt newborn caribou, too. In fall, they eat all the berries they can get their paws on.

As wilderness becomes rare, grizzlies and people are forced to share the same space. Grizzlies regard campers and their picnic baskets as trespassers or prey, which can lead to some grizzly encounters. Their attacks on people are rare, but when they occur they're brutal. Park rangers have tried relocating aggressive bears but the bears' strong homing instinct directs them back. When this happens the bears must be destroyed.

How would you save grizzlies, wolverines and other carnivores? Turn their habitat into parks and keep people out? Then what would happen to farmers, lumberjacks, miners and tourists? What about what they want? The United Nations thinks countries should set aside 12 percent of their land and water as wilderness for wildlife. Right now about 7.5 percent of the U.S. is set aside, mostly in Alaska. How would you convince adults to protect more wilderness?

47

WILDLIFE AND PEOPLE — UNEASY NEIGHBORS

The Wildlife Control truck stops in front of the neighbor's house. Out jumps a person dressed like a soldier, wearing protective gear from head to foot. She arms herself with a net on a stick and a cage, ready to do battle with another unwelcome guest — a raccoon. When she's finished here, her next stop will be the off-ramp of the expressway where a skunk has been run over by a trailer truck. What a job — evicting unwanted animals and cleaning up road kill.

Clashes between humans and wildlife are everyday sights in a big city. But there are also things happening between people and wildlife that you don't see. Look around the outskirts of your community for changes that have been made in the last year. Perhaps there's a new subdivision or golf course where a farm used to be, or warehouses on drained marshland by a lake. On every front, humans are encroaching on wildlife habitats.

 ildlife close-up: The panda

One thousand wild giant pandas live in Szechwan, China, a province about the size of New Brunswick or Maine. The pandas are protected in 12 government reserves located on the sides of mountains. These mountainside reserves are surrounded by farms and villages, like islands of wilderness in a sea of civilization. And that's the problem.

Each panda requires about 250 acres (100 ha) of bamboo forest to meet its needs for space, food and shelter. There is just enough room for the pandas in the reserves — unless disaster strikes. Every 50 or 60 years, the bamboo flowers and dies. Without warning, the pandas' food supply vanishes. In the past, when the bamboo died, the pandas would simply move on and find more. But today they cannot move; they are surrounded by humans on all sides.

The Chinese are proud and protective of their national symbol, the giant panda. When the bamboo dies, local people rush to save starving or orphaned pandas. Stranded bears are airlifted to other forests or nursed in special panda hospitals. With the help of international researchers, local people hope to find a way for pandas and people to live together in Szechwan.

SURVIVAL SCHOOL

What about wildlife that survive and even thrive near humans? Some birds nest in the eaves of houses. And raccoons prowl city alleys and rummage through garbage in search of food. They have learned to adapt to city life.

Can you figure out which of these animals would survive if their wilderness home were turned into a city suburb? Read the descriptions carefully. They'll give you some clues. Then check your answers on page 96.

Blue jay

Not afraid of people. Screams loudly and alerts the whole neighborhood when danger approaches. Eats insects, nuts and fruits common in oak forests, but will scavenge most anything — even dog food. Will it survive in the city?

Panda Droppings May Hold Clue to Survival

Don Reid, a scientist from Calgary, Alberta, works in Wolong, one of the 12 panda reserves in China. He radio-collared and tracked pandas, monitoring their movements. He also collected their droppings to learn what kind of bamboo they prefer. His work, which was funded by WWF, helped the Chinese authorities restore and protect the type of bamboo and forest home the pandas need.

Leopard frog

Lurks in swamps and meadows wet enough to keep its sensitive skin moist at all times. Expert at catching insects. In springtime, the females must find a pond in which to lay their eggs. Will it survive in the city?

Timber rattlesnake

Well-camouflaged. Eats mice and other woodland rodents. Venomous bite makes it the most poisonous of all northern snakes, so is feared by people. In winter, hundreds sleep together in great knots in caves and crevices. Will it survive in the city?

Common daisy

Pretty flowering plant that grows in sunny spots. Prefers poor soil that has been recently disturbed. Will it survive in the city?

Brook trout

Lives in clear, fast-running streams. Needs lots of oxygen. Eats insect larvae and flies. Will it survive in the city?

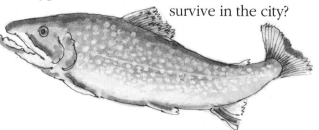

49

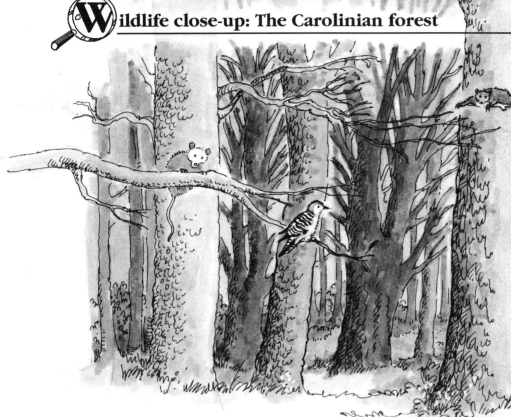ildlife close-up: The Carolinian forest

Yes, forests can be threatened by people, too. In the northeastern United States, farms and cities are gobbling up hardwood forests. As trees are cut to make room for fields, roads, and highrises, many plant and animal species that live there are threatened too. Over ninety-nine percent of the original forests are gone since the first settlers arrived. While some areas have been replanted or grown back, the forests and the wildlife that depend on them are caught in a human encroachment squeeze.

Wildlife close-up: Wild about golf

Many animals' homes are threatened when cities grow. Even a green and treed golf course will change things: sunny mown fairways are very different from shaded leafy woodlands. Some animals do browse on golf course grass, but those who like berries, nuts and twigs must go somewhere else. The places animals use for shelter, or to nest, burrow and den, change too. Animals that have adapted to live in marshes and flowing streams won't have a home when the swamps are drained and the creeks are dammed to make water traps for the golfers. What seem like small or ordinary changes to us can have big consequences for wildlife. Many animals will be driven away; some will die.

50

Fright Distances

Wild animals like to keep a safe distance between themselves and people. Scientists call this space the animal's fright distance. You can measure the fright distances of wild birds with a few simple props.

You'll need:

bird seed, breadcrumbs or bacon bits
a measuring tape or stick
a colored cloth or handkerchief
a bird guide for identifying (optional)

1. Visit a spot where there are wild birds, such as a neighborhood bird feeder in winter.

2. Sprinkle bird seed on the ground at different distances from you. Put the first handful 7 feet (2 m) away, the second 16 feet (5 m) away and the third 33 feet (10 m) away.

3. Watch. How close will the birds come to you? Try waving the handkerchief and see if that makes a difference.

4. Try the same experiment on various species of birds. Which are the shyest? Compare their fright distances.

5. Use the same feeder over several days and see if any of the birds get used to you and move closer. Can you figure out which birds wouldn't be threatened by people moving in nearby and which would?

WHAT'S WILD IN THE WEST?

Remember the old cowboy song

> Give me a home, where the buffalo roam
> And the deer and the antelope play...

Finding a home for the buffalo to roam is mighty hard these days. The truth is, the Wild West is one of the most endangered spaces on earth.

The North American west is made up of at least four prairie habitats: tall-grass prairie, mixed prairie, fescue prairie and aspen parkland. Each habitat has its own special plants and animals — and its own special problems.

Wildlife close-up: The tall-grass prairie

When settlers moved into the west just over 100 years ago, they found millions of acres (hectares) of grass and flowers so tall that people on horseback could ride through without being seen.

Under these fields lay a thick layer of roots, called sod. These roots could weigh three times as much as the plants that grew from them. When farmers plowed up the tall grasses to make crops, they discovered that the sod enriched the soil. It didn't take long for sodbusters — the farmers' nickname — to turn the tall-grass prairie into some of the best farming country.

Today, most of the tall-grass prairie is corn and wheat fields. The few patches that remain are on right-of-ways for roads, railways and power lines.

Many tall-grass animals have also disappeared. The plains grizzly and plains wolf are extinct. The swift fox and the greater prairie chicken are extirpated in Canada and in trouble in the U.S. Millions of plains bison once roamed the grasslands, but now survive in only a few, fenced-in herds. Even the butterflies that flitted among the tall grasses are rarely seen now.

Conservationists are working hard to identify the last stands of tall-grass prairie and protect them. From Texas to Manitoba, local groups have Prairie Patron programs to collect donations and buy up prairie land to ensure that it remains wild.

Grassroots Action

The province of Manitoba once had 1.5 million acres (600,000 ha) of tall-grass; now there are only 250 acres (102 ha) left, divided into 22 patches. One 25 acre (10 ha) patch is ringed with buildings in downtown Winnipeg.

A Winnipeg school class realized that without a tall-grass habitat, tall-grass animals would have no home. So they decided to plant a prairie themselves. The kids persuaded the tenants of a new senior citizens' complex that their backyard would look beautiful landscaped as a tall-grass prairie. Together the kids and the seniors collected seeds from a patch of wild prairie and planted a tall-grass habitat. Now the senior citizens have a garden of colourful, sweet-smelling flowers and waving grasses to walk in all summer long and tall-grass birds and butterflies have a home. Want to plant your own prairie? See below.

Grow Your Own Prairie — Even If You Don't Live There

The seeds of tall grasses and other prairie plants are available from many nurseries and seed catalogs. Use them to start a prairie garden in your own back yard. Here's what to look for:

Grasses: big bluestem, little bluestem, green needle grass, tall dropseed

Flowers: Canada anemone, cut-leaf anemone, dwarf false indigo, goat's-beard, golden alexander, meadow blazing-star, prairie crocus, tall cinquefoil, three-flowered avens, wild bergamot, purple and white prairie clover

1. Choose a sunny spot for your prairie garden (on the prairies there are few trees for shade). Carefully dig out all the weeds and break up the soil so it's loose to a depth of at least 1 foot (about 30 cm).

2. Follow the instructions on each package for planting. Most seeds sprout faster if you soak them in water overnight before planting.

3. Cover the soil with wet newspaper after planting to keep the seeds moist until they germinate.

4. When you see the first shoots, remove the paper. Protect the seedlings from too much hot sun and wind until the first strong leaves appear. To do this, punch holes about the size of a quarter all over the bottom of a cardboard box and turn the box over the seedlings.

5. Plant a variety of species together, just as in a wild prairie. Once they're growing well, the garden will look after itself. The plants will reseed each year and the old stalks will provide shelter for the new seedlings.

53

Wildlife close-up: The short-grass prairie

Although sodbusting destroyed most of the tall-grass prairie, poor water and soil care now threaten the health of the mixed prairie, fescue prairie and aspen parkland habitats.

The prairies have been thirsty for years. Early farmers drained prairie wetlands to make more farm fields. There seemed to be so much swamp water that it didn't matter. But soon, hunters noticed there weren't as many ducks each fall — with fewer wetlands, there were fewer places for the ducks to nest. And farmers found their fields dried out quickly when the wetlands were drained. Today, wise farmers have stopped draining the prairie and are letting previously drained areas fill with water again. Then they have the water their crops and cattle need, and ducks and other wildlife have nesting habitats.

Farmers have found they need to take care of prairie soil, too. The old practice of growing the same crop on the same field year after year weakens the soil, and grasshoppers and other pests move in to attack crops. If farmers use chemical fertilizers to nourish the soil and chemical pesticides to kill the insects, they accidently cause problems for wildlife. After the chemicals have done their work, they don't just go away. Some dissolve in rainwater, trickle along the ground as "run-off" and finally collect in lakes and wetlands. Scientists suspect wild animals get poisoned by drinking the water or by eating the plants and creatures that live in the water. One pesticide — carbofuran — is blamed for killing mallard ducklings, deforming young snapping turtles and poisoning burrowing owls.

Many farmers want to cut down on their use of chemicals in order to help wildlife and people. They're trying natural ways to keep their soil healthy and fight insects, too. One way they've found is crop rotation. By growing different crops on their fields each year, the soil doesn't get weak and tired, and the bugs that feed on specific plants don't increase in numbers. Another new farming method is called zero-tillage. If farmers don't plow under the stubble (leftovers from previous crops), the old stems and roots compost and fertilize the fields naturally. The stubble also keeps the soil from drying out and that helps the farmers' crops grow better. With crop rotation and zero-tillage, the soil improves and the crops stay healthy without the use of chemicals and the threat to wildlife habitat.

Finding cures like these for all threats to prairie habitat is important. Whether it's tall- or short-grass prairie, too much is disappearing or dying. Today, one-third of the birds and mammals listed as vulnerable, threatened and endangered in Canada comes from prairie habitat.

Wildlife close-up: Wetlands are soakers

Wetlands go by many different names: sloughs, quagmires, muskeg, swamps, marshes, waterholes, bogs, bayous or fens. Sometimes wetlands don't look very wet, but walk through one and you're in for wet feet.

Wetlands act as storage basins for water. In heavy rain, they absorb extra water like giant sponges and release it slowly. Wild animals know they can find a drink in a wetland, even if the land around is dried out.

Wetland water is home to countless microscopic creatures, as well as a variety of plants, insects, minnows, frogs and shellfish. Most birds feed on wetland wildlife for part of their lives; some, such as ducks and waders, depend entirely on wetland habitats. Many ocean and freshwater fish spawn in wetlands and the young feed and hide in the rich plant cover.

Wetlands are in trouble because people don't treat them well. Garbage and chemicals are dumped into the water. People even drain wetlands in order to build homes or grow crops. Today, one-third of the endangered and threatened species in the United States lives in wetlands.

Prairie or Great Plains Animals in Trouble

The following prairie or great plains animals are listed as threatened or endangered in the United States:

Mammals:
prairie dog
black–footed ferret
gray wolf
grizzly bear
ocelot

Birds:
Attwater's greater prairie chicken
red–cockaded woodpecker
American peregrine falcon
Arctic peregrine falcon
bald eagle
black capped vireo
eskimo curlew
least tern
piping plover
whooping crane

Fish:
beautiful shiner
bonytail chub
pallid sturgeon

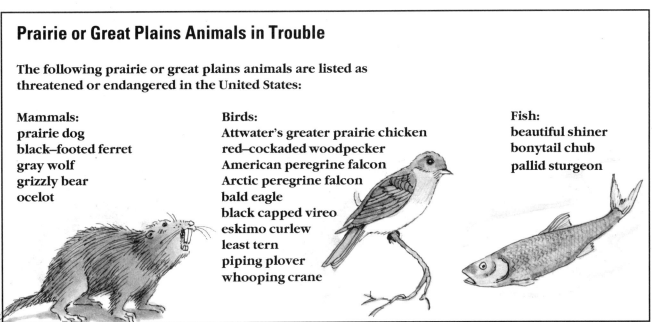

TIMBERRRR!

In January 1989, the kids at Brockton High School in Toronto, Ontario decided to do something about the mountain of scrap paper their school produced every week. They decided to recycle it and help save Canadian forests. The Paper Recycling Club took root. Every day their recycling team met at lunch. They picked up the school's waste paper and sorted it into bins for collection. Every two weeks, the Board of Education trucked away 350 pounds (160 kg) of paper for recycling.

Recycling didn't make money for the school, but it saved trees. Four average-sized spruce trees are needed to make the 265 pounds (120 kg) of paper used by every person in North America each year. Imagine how big a forest could be saved if more paper was recycled.

Preserving forests is important for wildlife. Just one tree can be home to hundreds of insects, birds and mammals. Animals live at different levels of the forest, like dwellers in a tall tree house.

It makes sense to recycle paper and save forests, but we still need wood for houses

This old growth forest on North America's west coast has never been logged. Undisturbed for hundreds of years, it has everything from giant spruces to this year's saplings. These layers of growth provide food and shelter for a wide variety of wildlife.

and furniture. So some trees will continue to be cut down.

Logging companies have two choices when they plan to log a forest. They can either cut some of the trees or all the trees. Cutting some trees is called selective logging. The trees to be cut are tagged and then carefully removed, leaving the remaining forest to grow.

The other way is clear-cut logging. Using bulldozers and chain saws, loggers cut or knock down every single tree, whether it is wanted for lumber or not. The choice trees are then hauled away and cut into planks for home building and furniture. The poorer quality wood may be left to rot or may be removed and used for products such as newspaper, cardboard boxes or pressboard. Clear-cut logging is an easier and cheaper way to harvest trees than selective logging. That's why logging companies prefer to clear-cut habitat.

There are many wildlife species that need a natural woodland — that means a messy one with live trees, dead trees and rotting trees. These animals and plants are threatened by the logging industry.

Why Say "No" To Clear-cutting

1. Clear-cutting removes more than trees from a habitat. The yearly carpet of soggy leaves goes when the trees go. Without this autumn carpet, the topsoil underneath can lose its grip. During spring run-off or in a heavy rain, the rich soil washes away.

2. Clear-cut mountainsides are difficult to reforest. Water and landslides pull the soil downhill, leaving bare, rocky slopes above and choking the rivers below.

3. Wind picks up speed over an expanse of clear-cut. Trees left standing can be blown down. Topsoil can be blown away.

4. Replanted saplings suffer from lack of moisture and steady winds.

5. Clear-cutting destroys nine times more trees than are needed.

6. Clear-cutting destroys wilderness. Logging roads, equipment and workers chase away wildlife that need peace and quiet.

7. Clear-cutting destroys habitats at all levels.

8. In 1991, U.S. federal, state, and private forests were harvested at a rate of approximately one football field (1.3 acres) every 5 hours.

CLEAR-CUT VICTIMS

You'd never see all these animals together in the same forest. They come from different parts of North America. You'd be lucky to spot a pine marten in Newfoundland or a marbled murrelet on the Pacific coast — they're endangered. They will become extinct if their forest homes are clear-cut. The other species — snowshoe hare, lynx and cicada — are threatened by clear-cut logging. If clear-cutting continues, all these species could be lost.

Newfoundland pine marten

To survive, this weasel-like animal needs fallen logs, up-rooted trees, piles of leaves and rotting stumps. In winter, this untidy habitat is covered with an insulating blanket of snow. The pine marten burrows in and feeds on rodents. It cannot live in cleared woods or even forests that have been replanted after logging. It's old-growth or nothing.

Marbled murrelet

Like many west coast sea-birds, the marbled murrelet spends its life at sea. Once a year it flies inland — at night — and lays its eggs in the rainforest either on the forest floor or in the old trees. It needs the privacy and shelter provided by the untidy tangle of underbrush.

Cicada

Most insects spend part of their lives underground. The cicada spends 17 years beneath the surface, in a larva state, feeding on the deep roots of old trees. When the larvae mature, they erupt from the soil all at once. They live above ground for only a few weeks, just long enough to lay eggs for the next generation.

Lynx

The body of the lynx is specially adapted to life in old-growth forests. Its long legs and big padded paws allow it to spring through deep snow, and it has no tail to slow it down. Its tufted ears are designed to pick up the muffled footsteps of the snowshoe hare. Although it is a skilled and successful predator in the woods, its padded paws slow it down in open country. There, unable to catch prey, it will starve.

Snowshoe hare

This hare doesn't hibernate. Its big feet act like snowshoes in winter and allow it to bound across the deep snow of the forest floor. Hiding in the hemlocks, the snowshoe hare listens with big ears, to hear a hungry lynx's quiet footsteps in the snow.

Environmental Posse

The kids at Brockton High in Toronto, Ontario, decided recycling was not enough. They held an adopt-a-tree program in the spring of 1990. Six hundred "orphan" white spruce seedlings, complete with planting instructions, were adopted by suitable families. This reforestation was free — the seedlings were donated.

A SPILL TO CRY OVER

Knock over a glass of milk and you know what to do: run for a dishcloth to wipe it up. Spilled milk is easy to clean. But what about spilled oil? When an oil tanker runs aground and spills its gooey guts into the ocean, there's no simple clean-up. The oil slick spreads, destroying marine habitat and killing many animals in the process.

Oil can be churned and whipped into what crews call chocolate mousse or it can glob together into sticky tarballs. Some oils sink; others float. Waves can splash the oil on shore and tides can take it out to sea. No matter where the oil ends up, it will affect everything in its path — from seaweed to plankton to grey whales, even grizzly bears walking along a beach.

Birds are visible victims of oil spills. Oil can get under their feathers and weigh them down until they drown. Or the oil makes their feathers matted and sticky, robbing the birds of their natural insulation. In cold ocean water it doesn't take long for oil-covered birds to freeze to death. Oil can also blind birds and cause breathing problems, arthritis, even stomach aches.

When the tanker *Exxon Valdez* spilled its oil into the Alaskan waters, murres that had gathered in noisy colonies to breed were coated with oil and thousands died. Those that made it to shore poisoned themselves by swallowing oil as they preened their feathers. Then they became deadly food for bald eagles.

Sea otters — the only sea mammal without a layer of blubber — rely on dense fur coats for warmth. Even a thin layer of oil can mat their fur, allowing frigid water to chill them. Then the otters freeze to death. Like seabirds, they frantically try to clean themselves, eating toxic oil in the process. Swallowed oil damages their kidneys, liver and stomach. Even otters that are rescued and cleaned up may die of illnesses caused by swallowing oil.

Fish drown in oil. Their gills get coated and they suffocate. Fish are at greatest risk for the first few days after a spill when the water is thick with toxins and tarballs. If an oil spill happens in spring, fish eggs and larvae floating on the surface can be poisoned too, killing an entire generation.

Fish that survive seem to be able to rid their bodies of the oil poisons. Only eight months after the *Exxon Valdez* spill, salmon tested safe for eating. But mussels, crabs and clams that live in the ocean floor and tidal flats take longer to recover.

Oil tankers cross the seas because people demand energy and oil products. Use less oil and there'll be fewer tankers and fewer chances of accidents. How can you and your family reduce the amount of oil you use? Form car pools, or take a bicycle to reduce gasoline use. And cut down on oil products such as heating oil, glue, detergents, insecticides, dyes, synthetic fibers, plastics, varnish, paints and lubricants.

You may think that changing a few habits won't help the otters or the cormorants. Think again. More birds die every year from slow and steady oil pollution that happens every day than are killed in massive oil spills. Little by little, people are wrecking the oceans — the largest habitat on earth. Changing our habits can help change the future.

Oil Invasion
You can see the damage oil does to bird eggs with this simple experiment.

You'll need:
1 cup (250 ml) vegetable oil
food coloring
a bowl
4 hard-boiled eggs
a kitchen timer or watch

1. Mix the oil and the food coloring together in a bowl in the sink.
2. Add the eggs.
3. Using a timer or watch, take one egg out of the mixture every 5 minutes.
4. Shell each egg when you take it out and slice it open to see if the oil has invaded the egg.

How long does it take for the oil to seep into the shell? Imagine what happens to bird eggs in the wild after an oil spill.

Cleaning Up After an Oil Spill

Volunteer clean-up crew members wear rubber gloves and boots, and their oldest clothes. They use pails, rakes, shovels, slotted spoons, garbage bags, nets, even paper towels to mop up oil on the shore.

Powerful cold-water hoses blast oil off the rocks and into the sea. The oil is captured by skimmers for recycling.

"Slicklickers" help clean up where a thick film of oil has collected. The machine slurps the oil off the top of the water, chugs it up a conveyor belt and plops it into a recycling container on a barge.

Collected waste is stored in garbage bags and burned in hospital incinerators or buried in toxic-waste dumps.

Aided by a cherry-picker, a trained crew blasts oiled cliffs with water heated to 617°F (325°C). This practice cleans off the oil but kills tiny organisms that live along the seashore.

When the water is calm, oil spills can be contained by booms. Booms float on the water, with a skirt or net under the water. Working around the edge of the booms are boats called skimmers, equipped with fancy vacuum cleaners that skim oil off the surface of the water.

Clean-up experts, wearing face masks and astronaut-like gear, spray a fertilizer on oiled beaches. This puts oil-eating bacteria to work, munching on the sticky shore.

Death at Sea

Oil accounts for only a small part of the pollution in the sea. Here are some other ocean killers:

• Plastic bags and bottles dumped into the oceans kill wildlife. Sea turtles die eating plastic bags, which they mistake for jellyfish, their favorite prey. Drifting plastic fishing nets kill thousands of dolphins and northern fur seals each year. Fish in the St. Lawrence River die from eating elastic bands that end up in the river off packets of mail.

• Poorly treated human sewage pours into lakes and rivers and eventually ends up in the ocean. It acts like fertilizer, making algae in the water grow rapidly. As algae blanket the surface, fish below smother from lack of oxygen.

• Chemicals, such as PCBs, mercury, cadmium (from batteries) and DDT, wind up in the oceans. They poison beluga whales and other marine mammals. Chemicals flow into the sea in rain and run-off from the land or are dumped deliberately off ships.

• Coral reefs, home to thousands of sea creatures, are under attack. Explosives and poisons are used to harvest tropical fish bound for aquariums. Many fish die in the process. The reefs, normally very colorful, are bleaching a dull white. Scientists don't know why, but suspect the rising water temperatures associated with the greenhouse effect and polluted run-offs along coastlines. Bleaching threatens to destroy the delicate and complex ecosystem of coral reefs.

Catching and punishing polluters of the oceans is very difficult. Beyond the 200 mile (300 km) limits claimed by most countries are international waters where there are no rules or rulers.

ACID RAIN — THE SILENT KILLER

This lake is chock full of plants and animals. Look closely and you can count 20 different species in and around the lake. (Turn to page 96 to see who's who.) Plants and animals live at different levels in the lake: some dwell in the muddy bottom, others in the depths or near the surface and still others around the shoreline. You can't quite see to the bottom in this healthy lake.

This is the same lake, after acid rain has fallen in it for several years. Where are all the plants and animals?

The fish gradually disappeared because fish eggs can't hatch in acidified lakes. The adult fish died off when tiny bits of metals were carried by acid rain out of the soil that surrounds the lake. The metals clogged the fish's gills and suffocated them.

Frogs, toads and salamander eggs were wiped out one spring by acid shock. This happened when acid that had built up in snowbanks flooded into the lake in one big poisonous dose with the spring melt.

As many of the lake-dwellers disappeared, so did the animals that depended on them for food. Today the lake is a silent place. Not even algae live in the water. When the lake started to die, some algae grew; but now that the lake is dead, it shines with an eerie clearness.

What causes acid rain and how can it be stopped? Turn the page to find out.

Acid Rain Witches' Brew

Acid rain is just ordinary rain mixed with pollution. People make pollution. Not me, you say? You're no polluter?

Sure, you don't deliberately make pollution. But every time you ride in a car, chemicals from the exhaust are pumped up into the air. Turning up the heat in your room or switching on a light uses energy. Energy made from fossil fuels pollutes twice — where the energy was made and again up your chimney. And every time you buy something that has been manufactured, you contribute pollution to the air because manufacturing makes pollution.

Pollution is brewed in coal-burning power plants, steel smelters and vehicle engines. And it is spit into the air through chimneys and tailpipes. Two of the most harmful pollutants are sulphur dioxide and nitrous oxide. These chemicals travel by air and fall to earth as acid rain, snow, mist or dust.

Stopping acid rain means stopping pollution. How can you help? Cut down on the energy you use. Can you think up ten ways to do this? Try it and see, then turn to page 96 for some ideas that other kids have come up with.

Acid Rain Fighters

- **In October 1990, the U.S. and Canada signed the Clean Air Act to reduce air pollution and acid rain.**

- **Scientists have discovered that microscopic bacteria live in lakes that appear dead. They feast on the acid that killed off the frogs and other aquatic life. Eventually, fish can be reintroduced, bringing with them birds and mammals. The lake will never have the same diverse life it once had but it will get a second chance.**

How Acid Is the Rain in Your Area?

Go to the kitchen and find a bottle of vinegar or a lemon. Sprinkle a small drop of vinegar or lemon juice on your finger and taste it. Do your lips pucker? Vinegar and lemon juice are acids. They are super-strong versions of acid rain.

Acids such as lemon juice or vinegar are at one end of a scale called the pH scale. At the other end of the scale are "bases." Ammonia and Milk of Magnesia are bases. Right in the middle of the scale are things that are neither acid nor bases — they're neutral.

Pure, "healthy" rain should be almost neutral — in the middle of the pH scale.

Here's how to find out how acid your rain is by using a red cabbage "indicator."

You'll need:
rainwater
 small, clean glass jars
a knife
a fresh red cabbage
boiling tapwater
measuring spoons
liquids to test (try tapwater,
    7-Up, dish soap mixed with water,
    vinegar, Milk of Magnesia)
an eye dropper

1. Collect rainwater in one of your jars. You don't need much — $\frac{1}{2}$ cup (125 ml) will do.
2. Ask an adult to help you cut the cabbage into small shreds. Stuff the shredded cabbage into a jar and cover it with boiling tapwater. Let it stand for two to three hours. This will be your acid indicator.
3. Pour 1 tablespoon (15 ml) of one of the test liquids into a small glass jar. Wash the measuring spoon and dry it, then put the second test liquid into another small jar. Continue putting each test liquid into a separate jar. Make sure you wash and dry your measuring spoons between liquids. Finish by putting 1 tablespoon (15 ml) of your collected rainwater into one of the small glass jars. Label each jar with what's inside it.
4. Use the eyedropper to add five drops of acid indicator (cabbage juice) to the first small jar. Watch for a reaction.

Acids turn pink when cabbage juice is added. Bases turn blue-green. Neutrals, like pure water, turn purple. How acid was the rainwater? If it's more pink than purple, it's acid rain.

You can take your project one step further. If you have a pen pal in another region, share this experiment with them and compare your results. Repeat your experiment in six months' time and see if the rain is less or more acidic. If it is more acidic, write your government and remind them about the Clean Air Act.

TEMPERATURE RISING: THE GREENHOUSE EFFECT

Ever walked into a greenhouse wearing a heavy coat? Pretty soon you're sweltering and sweating. What makes a greenhouse hot, even in winter? Light energy from the sun shines through the windows, turns into heat and gets trapped inside by the glass. Soon the temperature soars — good for tropical plants, but not for you in your heavy coat.

The earth itself is a bit like a huge greenhouse. Light from the sun enters the atmosphere and changes to heat. Some of that heat is held near the earth's surface by clouds and layers of gases to keep us warm. But most of the heat escapes back into space so we don't get too hot.

However, when people drive cars, burn Styrofoam or turn on the furnace or air conditioner, they add more heat-trapping gases to the atmosphere. These gases prevent heat from escaping, and so, slowly, the earth warms up. This gradual warming is called the "greenhouse effect."

Scientists fear the average temperature of the earth may rise nearly 6 degrees Fahrenheit (3 degrees Celsius) in the next 50 years. Three degrees doesn't sound like much, but warming in the Arctic regions will be two to three times greater than in the tropics. That's enough to melt the polar icecaps, which could put much more water into the

Black spruce trees are "waterproofed:" they're small and have short, tough needles so the winter wind can't rob their moisture. Black spruce grow in wet bogs so that they can suck up and store enough moisture to survive the frozen winters.

In summer, moose eat the mineral-rich roots of water plants. In winter, they live on forest edges, browsing on shrubs, twigs and bark — not a nourishing diet even for moose. In some places, moose can't move south to find better food because deer who live there carry a disease that is fatal to moose.

oceans, causing the sea level to rise almost 7 feet (2 m).

If the seas rose, water would flood into coastal marshes and river deltas, wiping out the homes of the animals who live there. In many cases, these animals wouldn't be able to find new homes farther inland because of towns and cities blocking their way.

While coastal habitats will be flooded, some wildlife habitats will be turned into deserts as the temperature increases. The northern forests of Canada and Alaska will become drier, more desert-like. What will happen to wildlife species adapted to today's cold winters and short, cool summers?

Try predicting the fates of these northern forest species. Will they survive the hot, dry climate the greenhouse effect will bring? (Turn to page 96 and see if your predictions are right.)

Red squirrels guard their territory and food supply with shrill calls. In the north, they hoard spruce and pine seeds in huge caches, called middens, for eating in the harsh winter. Red squirrels who live farther south, on the edge of grey squirrel territory, have learned to divide their seeds into several caches to protect the food from hungry grey squirrels.

The least weasel has a brown coat that turns white in winter, so it's difficult for predators to see it in the snow. It scoots under the snow along tunnels made by small rodents, catches prey and then moves the kill into an empty burrow. After dinner, it plucks the fur off its victim to insulate a corner of the burrow and then rolls up in a warm ball to sleep. It wakens again only when it's time for another meal.

Say No to Styrofoam

Kids in Tenakill, New Jersey, decided to cut down on pollutants that add to the greenhouse effect. They called themselves Kids Against Pollution and persuaded their school board to ban Styrofoam in the school cafeteria. When a national television show did a feature on their work, lots of other kids across America joined up.

Cathy, a seventh grade student, took their message to the United Nations. She told the experts that Kids Against Pollution were committed to stopping Styrofoam use. She pointed out that the committee members listening to her testimony were drinking coffee out of Styrofoam cups and adding to the problem.

Cathy reminded the United Nations that cars are some of the biggest offenders. One car can add a ton (tonne) of heat-collecting gases to the atmosphere every year.

WILDLIFE CLOSE-UP: THE RAINFOREST

It's Jungle in Here

Picture a tree ten stories high wrapped with vines as thick as a human body. Imagine a whole forest of these monster trees. Welcome to a rainforest, a tropical jungle. (To see who's who, turn to page 96.)

ORIOLES, TANAGERS, WARBLERS AND SWALLOWS NEST IN CANADA AND THE U.S. BUT MIGRATE TO THE RAINFOREST FOR THE WINTER. SO WHAT ARE THEY, NORTHERN OR RAINFOREST BIRDS?

RAINFORESTS GROW IN A NARROW BAND AROUND THE EQUATOR CALLED THE TROPICS. EVERY RAINFOREST HAS DIFFERENT PLANTS AND ANIMALS. THIS IS A COSTA RICAN LOWLANDS RAINFOREST.

RAINFOREST SOILS STAY AT A CONSTANT TEMPERATURE OF 86°F (30°C) — LIKE A WARM SWIMMING POOL.

A SMALL WOODLOT IN MICHIGAN HAS ABOUT 10 SPECIES OF TREES; THE SAME SIZED MALAYSIAN RAINFOREST WOULD HAVE 220 SPECIES.

SCIENTISTS FOUND ONE KIND OF TREE IN PANAMA THAT WAS HOME TO 1200 SPECIES OF BEETLES, 163 OF WHICH ARE FOUND NOWHERE ELSE.

TROPICAL FORESTS COVER ONLY 14 PERCENT OF THE LAND ON EARTH, BUT CONTAIN MORE THAN HALF OF THE WORLD'S SPECIES. MOST RAINFOREST PLANTS AND ANIMALS HAVE NEVER BEEN STUDIED AND HAVE NO NAMES.

Rainforests in Trouble

Sadly, rainforest trees are being cut down by the millions, endangering the plants and animals that live in them. In the time it takes you to read this sentence, an area of rainforest the size of a football field will have disappeared, probably forever. If rainforests continue to be destroyed at this rate, there will be no undamaged rainforests by the year 2070. Long before then, 60 000 plant species and more than a million animal species may become extinct.

Why are rainforests being cut down? Many African and Asian rainforests are logged for timber and pulp. The mahogany tree is endangered now and teak and ebony may be next. In Central America, some rainforests are burned to make cattle ranches for the fast-food hamburger market. In South America, new roads into mining developments and hydroelectric dams make it possible for farmers to get into rainforest areas that were once inaccessible. The farmers cut down and burn the forest to make way for farms alongside the road. Often these farmers find they have to move on after a few years. That's because rainforest soils are poor — the richness of rainforests is stored in the trees.

Scientists found 90 plants never before described in an area of Ecuador. The whole area was clear-cut after they left. The 90 plants vanished forever.

2·5 ACRES (1 HA) OF TROPICAL RAINFOREST SPROUTS 90 TONS (90 T) OF GREEN LEAVES A YEAR.

PLANTS LIVE ON PLANTS IN THE RAINFOREST. FOR MORE INFORMATION ABOUT THE BROMELIAD, TURN THE PAGE.

IF YOU COLLECTED ALL THE WATER THAT FALLS ON ONE LEAF IN THE RAINFOREST FOR ONE YEAR, YOU'D FILL A BATHTUB TO OVERFLOWING.

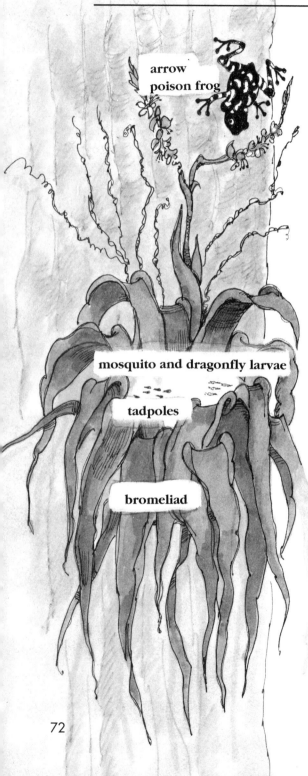

arrow poison frog

mosquito and dragonfly larvae

tadpoles

bromeliad

A single rainforest tree can be home to hundreds of wildlife species. Animals and plants live at various levels on the tree depending on how much they like sun or shade. This bromeliad (a spiky rainforest plant that resembles a pineapple) grows high up on the side of rainforest trees. Water gathers in the cup formed by its stiff leaves, making a pool large enough for the arrow poison frog to lay eggs in. The arrow poison tadpoles eat mosquito and dragonfly larvae living in the same pools. So the bromeliad is a micro-world of its own, high above the ground.

Rainforests are home to a rich variety of plants and animals. Scientists call this richness "biological diversity." Cut down just one rainforest tree and hundreds of fascinating creatures lose their homes.

Buy Yourself a Rainforest

You can help stop the destruction of rainforests by being a careful shopper.

• Before you order a hamburger at a restaurant, ask where the beef comes from. If the answer is from a rainforest country, such as Costa Rica, chances are nearly 24 square yards (20 square meters) of rainforest were destroyed to grow the beef for your burger.

• Rainforest beef shows up in TV dinners and in some brands of canned foods. If you use these products, find out where the beef comes from by reading the label or by writing the food packager. Ask your parents not to buy a product again if it contains rainforest beef.

• You can also help save rainforests by being careful about the wood your family buys. Ask your parents to avoid purchasing furniture made from rosewood, teak or mahogany. Even plywood may come from a rainforest area. Check before you buy. Some rainforest trees end up in chopsticks. Refuse to use disposable chopsticks.

Build a Rainforest Tree

Rainforest trees are unlike other trees. They have shallow roots and slender trunks, but they grow hundreds of feet (meters) tall. To support the height and weight of their trunks, many rainforest trees grow wide bases called stilts or buttresses. Try building a tall tree out of dry spaghetti and marshmallows. Does starting with a wide base help you build a taller tree? How tall a tree can you build in half an hour?

Use the marshmallows to join the spaghetti pieces together.

A TROPICAL RAINFOREST IN YOUR HOME

The tropical rainforest may be distant and wild, but it's part of our everyday life. Many common foods, medicines, even the weather outside our front door, depend on the jungle.

Destruction of rainforests threatens the plants and animals that live in the rainforest. It will also affect us.

Food from the Rainforest

A lot of the foods we eat come from plants that grow in rainforests. Serve your mother or father a tropical rainforest breakfast in bed. As your parent digs in, point out that all the foods originally came from rainforest countries and that they are constantly being improved by breeding with wild rainforest relatives.

• Corn and rice in breakfast cereals can fight off disease and frost better after they are bred with wild rainforest plants.

• Wild Indonesian sugar cane has improved its farm-grown cousin.

• Wild chocolate from Ecuador and wild coffee from Ethiopia have improved these two morning drinks.

• Regular oranges taste juicier after crossbreeding with a wild variety from Papua, New Guinea.

Health from the Rainforest

Four out of every ten medicines we use come from wild plants and animals. Most of these live in the rainforest.

• Tonic water, made from the bark of the cinchona tree, has long been used as a medicinal drink. Doctors found that quinine, a substance in the bark, protects people against malaria.

• For centuries, Amazon Indians used curare from the wild grape plant, to poison-tip their darts. Modern surgeons now use tubocurarine, derived from the same plant, as a muscle relaxant in open-heart surgery.

• The rosy periwinkle, a pretty flowering plant from Madagascar, increases resistance to leukemia in children.

• Fewer than 1 percent of rainforest species have been tested for use in modern medicine. The destruction of the rainforest may threaten development of potential medicines. That's why it makes sense to protect the rainforest. Our lives may depend on it!

Weather from the Rainforest

When a tropical forest is cut, rainfall in the immediate area declines. In Panama, where the forest was cut for cattle pasture 50 years ago, the annual rainfall has dropped more than $1\frac{1}{2}$ inches (4 cm) a year. There's not enough rain for ranching any more.

Scientists think cleared land reflects more heat and light into the atmosphere than forested land does. This changes wind and cloud patterns in the area and in nearby countries, too.

But worst of all, when the trees are cut they are usually burned. Smoke from fires adds to the pollution and worsens the greenhouse effect (see page 68). As the forest burns, rainforest animals lose their homes. So do animals in other parts of the world; their habitats are changed because of the greenhouse effect.

Left alone, leaves in a growing forest hold onto greenhouse gases and keep them from collecting in the air. The rainforest also stores precious fresh water in the trunks, branches and leaves of its trees and in the swirling clouds and dew all around. A healthy rainforest belt around the equator moderates the world's weather systems.

A South American tribal legend speaks true: "The tropical rainforest supports the sky. Cut down the trees and disaster follows!"

Write for the Rainforest

Ever wonder what big food and drug companies are doing to help save the rainforest? Why not write and ask? Tell them they need the rainforest to keep improving their products.

RAINFOREST ACTION FILE

Kids have invented all kinds of nifty ways to tell people about the rainforest and to raise money to help protect it.

Flying High

Sixth grade students in Elmira, Ontario, started a club they called the Amazon Air Machine. They turned their classroom into a tropical rainforest with huge paper tree trunks and creeping vines. The Amazon River even flowed along the ceiling! Every morning, they started school by singing the Brazilian national anthem. To get their families involved, the students made a deal with two local grocery stores to give the students a rebate on every $800 worth of purchases. By saving grocery store tapes, the school families raised $413.32 and donated it to the World Wildlife Fund to preserve 20 acres (8 ha) of rainforest.

The Junior — Senior Connection

Elementary school kids in Miami, Florida, wanted to involve others in their concern for the rainforest. They decided to work with a group of senior citizens and together they baked bread and potted plants. Then the kids and the seniors held a sale and donated the proceeds to the World Wildlife Fund to help save 8 acres (3.2 ha) of the tropical rainforest in Costa Rica.

A Walk on the Wild Side

Third form students from Tonbridge, Kent, produced rainforest posters and set them up in a "jungle walk" display at school. They cut out giant green leaves (from recycled paper) and sold them to parents and friends. The leaf buyers were asked to write their names on the leaves and stick them on the "jungle walls" to demonstrate their commitment to saving the rainforest. Leaf sales raised $108.71 to help save Cameroon rainforest.

Rainforest Snacks

Fifth grade students in King City, Ontario, raised $141.73 in a bake sale to protect 7 acres (3 ha) of rainforest forever. Here is one of their recipes. The ingredients rely on a growing rainforest, not a cut one.

Colin and Adrian's Food-from-the-Rainforest Squares

$\frac{3}{4}$ cup (175 ml) honey
1 cup (250 ml) peanut butter
1 cup (250 ml) semi-sweet chocolate chips
1 tsp. (5 ml) vanilla
1 cup (250 ml) peanuts
3 cups (750 ml) Rice Krispies

1. Melt the honey and peanut butter in the top of a double boiler.
2. Add the chocolate chips and mix until they are melted too.
3. Remove the double boiler from the heat and stir in vanilla, then the peanuts and then the Rice Krispies.
4. Press into a square cake tin. Slice when cool.

Now, bite into a hunk of rainforest richness!

Who Owns the Rainforest?

When kids donate money to World Wildlife Fund to help the rainforest, the kids don't "own" the acre. Neither does World Wildlife Fund.

In some countries, the money is used to buy rainforest so that it can be saved as government parkland. The Monteverde rainforest in Costa Rica was enlarged by this kind of "buying."

In other countries, the parks are already set aside, but there isn't any money to protect them. There are no wardens, no fences, no education programs. In these countries, the donated money goes to hiring local people and buying equipment to protect the park. Rainforest acres in Brazil, Mexico, Ecuador, Peru, Guatemala and Belize are protected in this way.

Local conservationists look after the rainforest treasures in their own countries, with the help of people from all over the world.

KIDS CAN MAKE A DIFFERENCE

That's what Dr. Kathy Blanchard found out. A scientist from Ipswich, Massachusetts, Dr. Blanchard is interested in saving seabirds on the North Atlantic coasts of Canada and the U.S. She found that seabirds are threatened from pollution and overfishing. Kathy also found they were hunted in large numbers by local people. And that wasn't helping seabirds at all. In some villages, it was a tradition to hunt seabirds for the family stewpot. This custom was passed on from generation to generation. Kathy tried talking to adults about stopping the hunt but got nowhere. So she talked to the kids and they got interested.

Kids persuaded their parents it was more fun to enjoy live seabirds than to eat dead ones. Some kids even performed plays about the problems seabirds face. Now most communities have reduced or stopped the hunt altogether.

Here are some wildlife problems that adult researchers are working on. Can you come up with a solution to help?

ildlife close-up: Florida panther

This small lion once prowled across the southeastern U.S. When ranchers settled the territory, some Florida panthers added livestock, particularly young horses, to their diet. That made the ranchers angry.

The ranchers discovered that Florida panthers were easy to kill because, when chased by dogs, they'd run a short distance and then climb a tree. The dogs' barking alerted ranchers, who arrived with their guns. Florida panthers were chased and killed in this way until their numbers fell to about 100, most of which lived in Everglades National Park.

Today, the U.S. Fish and Wildlife Service is trying to change people's attitudes towards the panther as well as reintroduce the cat to some of its old range. They want at least three healthy populations of panthers instead of one.

Can you think of ways to help change people's attitudes towards the Florida panther?

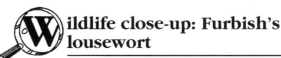ildlife close-up: Furbish's lousewort

A total of 5546 plants with this crazy name exist on earth — 5000 in Maine and 546 in New Brunswick. They all grow near a river that developers want to dam for hydroelectric power.

Ten years ago, conservationists stopped a billion dollar hydroelectric project in Maine because the dam threatened the Furbish's lousewort. Now, a New Brunswick plan to dam the river threatens nearly half the Canadian plants.

Can you suggest ways to help these plants?

Wildlife close-up: The leatherback turtle

The number of leatherback turtles is falling rapidly. Why? People know all of the leatherbacks' nesting beaches. They wait until the eggs are laid and then kill the adults for food. Afterward, they collect the eggs.

In Costa Rica and Malaysia, the nesting beaches are guarded and "farmed" so the harvest of eggs and adults is controlled. But other important beaches in the Caribbean, South Africa and New Guinea are not managed.

Leatherbacks have problems in Canada and the U.S. as well. Every year, some are caught in fishing nets off Newfoundland and Labrador. Most are still alive when hauled in, but don't make it if they're then towed to the wharf to be shown off to amazed on-lookers.

In the U.S., leatherbacks are found dead on New England beaches every year. It seems leatherbacks confuse floating plastic bags and bottles for their favorite food — jellyfish. Their insides clog up with human garbage and the huge turtles die.

How can kids help the leatherback?

ildlife close-up: The Puerto Rican crested toad

This toad has been snatched by collectors and its swampy home has been drained for farms and tourist hotels. So few were left that it was thought to be extinct. Then, in 1980, two teachers found several Puerto Rican crested toads in a cattle trough in Puerto Rico.

Zoos in Buffalo, New York, and Toronto, Ontario, got several of the toads and successfully mated them to produce thousands of toadlets. But releasing them into the wild has presented a problem. Only one known breeding site is still untouched by development. And somebody wants to pave it for a parking lot. Scientists are worried that if they designate the site a "critical habitat" to stop the parking lot, collectors will show up and start toad-napping again.

Have you any suggestions?

Is There an Endangered Species in Your Community?

If you don't know, phone your local naturalists' society and find out. Read about the animal to see how you can help. Tell your idea to parents and friends, and tell the naturalists' society, too. Adult wildlife workers need lots of new and good ideas.

ON YOUR OWN: A WILDLIFE-FRIENDLY LIFESTYLE

You can help save wildlife and wild habitats just by shopping wisely and thinking "green" around the house.

These ideas came from a group of kids in Richmond Hill, Ontario. The kids thought that if they were "wildlife responsible" in their own lives, they would set a good example for others. Can you think of more ways to be wildlife friendly?

SHOPPING

When shopping, think where your purchase comes from. Paper comes from trees, plastic is made from oil, metal is dug from mines, food grows on farms. Getting the basic material, transporting it, manufacturing it, packaging it and throwing it out — all affect wildlife and their habitat.

• Buy only what you need. Use less. Choose what will last!

• Take your own shopping bag to the store — you don't need another one.

• When choosing food, be suspicious of perfect-looking fruit and vegetables. They've probably been heavily sprayed with pesticides.

• Buy products in returnable or refillable containers. If they're not available, look for recyclable ones instead.

• Don't buy overpackaged goods. If you need the item, why not unwrap it when you get home and return it to the manufacturer along with your comments about excess packaging? Do candy bars need two layers of wrap?

• Be careful when you buy products that dissolve in water. Find out if the detergent or cleaner will kill wildlife once it's gone down the drain. Find out about safe alternative cleaners from your local environmental group.

• Do not buy anything that is made from an endangered species. This is important, especially when you travel to another country.

AT HOME

Waste

Before you throw something out, think where it will go—to an incinerator and add to air pollution, or to a dump and add to water pollution? Pollution hurts wildlife and wild habitat.

• Offer to help at home with the dishes and laundry. Then ask your family to give up using paper towels, paper plates, paper cups, disposable paper diapers and so on.

• Recycle bottles, jars, metal cans, newspapers and plastic containers. If you don't know where to take them, phone your municipal government and ask how you can recycle in your community.

• Start a compost pile and feed it with organic waste from the kitchen and garden — eggshells, fruit and veggie scraps, leaves and so on. After it's decomposed, you have a great soil conditioner to spread on your garden.

• Save stuff like egg cartons, baskets, buttons, and baby food jars for the kindergarten or daycare in your neighborhood for crafts. Pass on used clothes to local charities, disaster relief — and relatives.

• Guard against careless disposal of toxic materials — paint, batteries, cleaners, pesticides, motor oil, etc. Find out where it's safe to dispose of them in your community by phoning the public works department in your city or town.

Energy

Most of our home energy comes from burning fossil fuels. The process of burning adds to acid rain and the greenhouse effect — both destroyers of wildlife habitat.

• Turn off electrical appliances you aren't using — lights, TV, radio, computer.

• Make a quick choice from the fridge — don't stand and gaze, letting out the energy-cooled air.

• Hang wet clothes outside on a nice day and give the dryer a rest.

• Don't crank the furnace way up in winter or the air conditioner in summer — wear appropriate clothing and keep the thermostat at a sensible temperature.

Garden

Encourage wildlife to share the garden with you.

• Build a bird feeder and keep it stocked all winter long. How about a hummingbird feeder in summer?

• Build a bird house and a bat box. You can get instructions from a library.

• Plant onions, marigolds and garlic to keep insect pests away from your vegetable garden. Your garden center can suggest other plants as alternatives to pesticides. They can also help you identify insects that will help get rid of pests. Yes, lots of insects are gardeners' friends.

• Use your compost to fertilize. Then you won't need chemical fertilizers.

• Nurture trees and meadow plants in your garden to attract wildlife, naturally.

TRANSPORTATION

The family car is an environmentally expensive means of travel. Just think of what it's made of — metal, plastic, glass. The metal, for instance, is dug from mines often situated in wild areas. Then the ore is processed in smelters and refineries that contribute to air and water pollution. Once manufactured, the car runs on gas and oil, which are wildlife risky in their extraction and processing — pipelines, oil tankers, slicks. When you use the car, its exhaust contributes to acid rain and the greenhouse effect.

• Walk, bike or take public transportation when you can.

• Don't push for a fast, flashy family car. Think fuel efficiency, pollution-control devices, long use, minimum "extras."

• Help take care of the car. Keep it in good shape so it pollutes as little as possible.

• Avoid off-road motor vehicles — motorbikes, snowmobiles, ATVs. They gobble energy and trample habitat. Bike or cross-country ski instead.

TAKE-OUT TREATS

When you crave a take-out meal or snack, think how it affects wildlife. Is it packaged in a series of throwaway layers and containers that litter the environment, are difficult to recycle and clog the garbage systems? Was it grown originally in an endangered habitat — tall-grass prairie or cleared tropical rainforest?

• Speak to your favorite take-out restaurateur or variety store owner about recycling. How can they participate?

• Try new foods — maybe you'll find a taste you like that's less wildlife expensive.

• Try snacking at home. Buy in bulk — raisins, chips and so on — and eat out of a bowl instead of "handy," individual throwaway containers.

IN A GROUP: MORE WILDLIFE-FRIENDLY IDEAS

Kids in elementary school like to speak out on behalf of wildlife. And they can be inventive and effective spokespersons.

The more kids become informed about wildlife issues, the more they have ideas about how they can help. And when kids are able to contribute effectively, all the theory and knowledge they're learning becomes real for them. The kids feel good about themselves and their world's future.

The following pages outline ways for teachers, parents and group leaders to support the infectious enthusiasm that kids have as they learn about endangered species and habitat. Most of the ideas cited as examples actually germinated in the remarkable minds of kids themselves and were carried out successfully with a helpful adult in the background.

Taking That Project One Step Farther

In school and in youth programs, kids take on projects to earn marks or badges. Even though much of the work may be outstanding, the projects die after they've been completed, marked and shared within the group. Some projects may lie in a bedroom or on a refrigerator for a while, but they soon disappear.

Why not show the kids how to take their efforts one step farther? Let them go beyond defining wildlife issues and learn something about the processes for dealing with those issues.

At The Bush School in Seattle, high school students studied wetlands. The kids' research showed that the weed Purple Loosestrife was taking over local wetland habitat, threatening recreation lakes and waterfowl marshes. They measured how fast the weed spread and also the amount of petroleum in the water. They interviewed local politicians and sent their results to the state agriculture department. A wider audience was reached by sharing their findings with other schools. The kids were satisfied, knowing they'd informed other people about concerns they'd identified.

Primary students on Campobello Island, New Brunswick, learned about endangered species at the same time they learned how to sew. They created a beautiful patchwork quilt with each square illustrating a different animal in trouble. But when they'd finished, they didn't just fold up the quilt and put it on the bottom of some lucky person's bed. They donated it to the town library and held a public unveiling. Local politicians and press came to the event and many people heard about the kids' work and their concerns for wildlife. The kids have the continued satisfaction of knowing that their quilt conveys its message every day to people who use the library.

Next time your kids are working hard on wildlife projects, encourage them to think how they can take them one step farther.

Reinforcing Personal Lifestyle Changes

Kids in a group sometimes take on major lifestyle changes and have a lot of fun at the same time. The bigger the group involved, the bigger the visible results — and that gives the participants a great feeling. It sets a fine example for the community too. Encourage your group of kids to look over the suggestions for lifestyle changes on pages 82–85, and see what ideas they can come up with.

When the custodian of a school in King City, Ontario, pointed out that it took fewer than 200 kids to produce 11 large bags of lunch garbage a week, the kids decided to change their bad habits. For a week they examined what they were throwing out. One class made posters showing how these garbage items hurt people and wildlife and hung the posters in the hall. Another class made signs explaining recycling alternatives. A third class created ugly garbage monsters out of the lunch waste, invented names and life histories for them, and displayed the creatures in the lunch room. Then the principal sent a note home asking all families to join in trying to send garbageless lunches to school. The next day, the school started to record the week's count of bags. That week, the kids managed to go from 11 bags to three!

One youth group in Los Angeles, California, agreed that our throwaway society was a threat to people and wildlife. They decided that each member would carry all personal garbage in a pack on her or his back for a week. Only when the kids were asleep could they take their packs off, but even then, the garbage had to stay beside them. During the week, the kids found they needed to make choices in what they used in order to reduce their creation of garbage. They shared ideas on how to deal with food waste and garbage that smelled. At the end of the week, they dumped out their packs together and considered ways to cut their waste more.

Staging a Celebration of Wildlife

During Environment Week, National Wildlife Week or World Rainforest Week, kids love to stage a celebration. Some kids set up environment fairs with speakers, information booths, displays, films, games and contests. Others prepare dramatic or musical productions or art exhibits. There's lots of room for fun — try staging a survival fashion show (instead of furs and ivory jewellery, the kids make wacky fashions out of rummage and garbage) or a wild field day (competitors dress up as endangered animals).

Whatever your kids decide to try, here are some tips to help them make the event a success:

1. Phone TV, radio and newspaper people to let them know about the event. Deliver a press release to their offices several days ahead of time. Make sure to include a contact person's name and phone number on the press release.

2. Write a program and distribute it to the people who attend. List credits acknowledging the help of kids and others who have been important to the success of the event.

3. Plan for refreshments — even if only lemonade and coffee. This gives the audience and participants a moment to reflect, casually in groups, on the event.

Junior school students in Devon, England, took their concerns for the rhino onto their town's High Street. They wanted to celebrate what they called "the strange and terrifying beauty of the rhino" and at the same time tell the general public the story of the rhino's plight. So, with advance publicity to stir up interest and press releases to the local media, the students spent the day drawing rhinos on the pavement with chalk. Because their idea was good and they were well organized, the kids also raised more than $200 for the "Rhino Emergency Appeal."

The Write Stuff

Kids write letters expecting their concerns about wildlife will be heard. But letter writing often doesn't get satisfying results — perhaps only a glossy pamphlet or a lecture on litter. That can lead to a sense of powerlessness. Here's where a supportive adult can step in with suggestions that will cut down on the frustration.

Kids' letters get action if:

• They are addressed to the right person with copies to other interested parties, such as government officials and newspaper editors (get these names by phone).

• They are original, not form letters. Why not try a poem or a song?

• They aren't overly polite — passion helps.

•They are specific and detailed: "I am worried about brown, chemical pollution in the river that runs near my home," not, "I am worried about water pollution."

• They ask for an answer — "What are you going to do?"

Kids in Stratford, Ontario, found an effective way to use their letter writing. They read a letter to the editor in their local paper in which a woman complained that kids don't appreciate trees. The class happened to be studying the rainforest and had already shown their appreciation for trees in a big way by collecting money to protect an acre. So they wrote to the paper and pointed out why, as kids, they were concerned about trees and why they wanted the rainforest to still be there when they grew up. It was time more adults were showing concern, they wrote. Three of their letters and one piece of art were printed in the next issue of the paper. The kids had the satisfaction of knowing that many adult readers would learn from their letters about the importance of the rainforest.

Kids have also used writing skills effectively in creating a newsletter — an impersonal kind of letter. Fifth grade students in Milton, Ontario, produced one called the *Baldwin Times*. The kids wrote articles with punchy titles such as "Plant Smuggling Threatens Species," "Acid Rain Eating Away Our Buildings," "Chemicals in Niagara Mist," "The Endangered Eagle." Each article was signed by the writer. Copies of the newsletter, sold for five cents a copy, let others know about the kids' concerns.

International Kid Power

For international issues such as the greenhouse effect and acid rain, kids can compare the effects on their environment with kids in another region or country. They can correspond, swap photos or video accounts, even plan visits to each other's country.

High school students in York Region, Ontario, wanted to help with the major oil spill in Alaska. After much negotiation, they were able to go to the site to make a video of what they saw for students back home. This was a major undertaking, with fund-raising drives, negotiations with the Coast Guard, travel and billeting arrangements in a town already crowded with visitors and so on. However, it was a trip of a lifetime for those students, broadening their world view and that of the students they visited in Alaska.

Public Focus provides Grades 5, 6 and 7 and youth groups with a ready-made international acid rain monitoring project called BARK (Backyard Acid Rain Kit). A hundred and twenty thousand kids from ten Canadian provinces and 16 American border states are involved. Students or youth groups participate in monitoring pH levels, correspond with a twin class or group in the other country and submit their data to a central collection computer that, in turn, reports back the final results of the whole project. To find out more about BARK, write to Public Focus, 489 College St., Suite 500, Toronto, Ontario M6G 1A5.

Fund-raising

Fund-raising can be a very satisfying way for kids to help endangered wildlife and wild places. But the kids have to know their subject well enough to persuade others to join in their commitment. If they do, they can raise awareness among the contributors as well as cash.

Begin by engaging kids in a frank discussion of where they want their money spent. They should do some research to be sure their hard-earned cash goes to important research or environmental action, not to administrative expenses.

Sometimes kids like to know their money is going to be spent in a very concrete way. World Wildlife Fund, for instance, provides this funding "schedule:"

• $400 helps biologists breed peregrine falcons in captivity for release in the wild.

• $200 puts a biologist into the field to count beluga whales.

• $80 buys radio-tracking equipment needed to follow captive-bred swift foxes released into the wild.

• $40 creates some education material designed by the Inuit about the bowhead whale.

• $30 prints signs and posters to galvanize a local community to action protecting precious wolverine habitat.

• $20 provides colored leg bands for tagging burrowing owls so that we will know where they winter.

• $50 to $100 protects 1 acre ($\frac{1}{2}$ ha) of rainforest as a wild place.

One of the most popular ways for kids to raise money is through bake or popcorn sales at recess. A class that has studied endangered species advertises throughout the school with posters and morning announcements so everyone knows to bring cash. The kids predict how much food they will need in the sale and divide up the baking. They also calculate their costs so they can tally their total gross earnings and then find their net earnings after expenses have been subtracted. Everyone in the class bakes snack-sized portions the night before. It takes a chunk of the morning to set up the food and cash boxes in a good spot to catch customers. When the recess bell rings, the sale begins! Everyone in the class helps

Bake sales raise incredible sums of money. The Kids for Saving Earth Club in a Troy, Michigan, school netted $700 with monthly cupcake sales. Fourth graders in Whitby, Ontario, raised $76.08. Deerwood Elementary School in Kingwood, Texas, sold "rainforest crunch cookies," raising $400.

Other groups have held raffles, made and sold badges, printed and auctioned off boxer shorts, collected and sold used tennis balls, aluminum cans and egg cartons. And the list goes on!

Some energetic school kids hold fund-raising days in which they combine all sorts of activities. Students in Manson's Landing, British Columbia, got the use of the local community hall and held a raffle of local art, sold rainforest buttons, ran videos and sold refreshments. They raised $160 for the protection of the tropical forest.

A lot of work, but worth it!

Going All Out with a Theme Study

Lots of teachers choose themes to study during the year and approach them in an interdisciplinary way. Wildlife lends itself well to this method. Teachers can weave the study of endangered species, for instance, into the spelling, reading, geography, mathematics, science, creative writing, art, music and even phys-ed programs for the duration of the unit.

Some teachers take the method to extremes; with endangered species, this can be "wildly" successful. One class in Scarborough, Ontario, started a unit on whales by creating a half-size (to scale) adult blue whale out of wire and papier mâché and then hanging it from the ceiling of the classroom. After this hands-on start, the kids had no difficulty immersing themselves in the unit. Big Blue was the subject of school-wide interest and the kids constantly had visitors with whom to share their knowledge and concerns about whales.

A study of the rainforest lends itself to an in–depth interdisciplinary study too. Kids in Watertown, Connecticut, turned their classroom into a steaming jungle, including carpeting–tube trees with crepe paper leaves, cotton moss, yarn vines, spiders, snakes, humidifier mist, fish in a river viewed from a real bridge, and wood chips on the floor. Kids studied to become certified tour guides and accepted donations for their tours. They also raffled off a bromeliad and sold rainforest candies to protect acres of rainforest. The project received national attention when WWF filmed their presentation for T.V. news.

Next time you start a wildlife unit, think big — your efforts could get others interested in working to save wildlife!

GLOSSARY

Biological diversity the wealth and variety of life on earth

Conservation the management of all human use of the natural world so that both present and future people may benefit from it

DDT a pesticide. DDT is a short form of its full name, dichlorodiphenyltrichloroethane

Delisted describes a species that is no longer considered to be vulnerable, threatened, endangered or extirpated

Down-listed describes a species that has recovered so that it is considered to be in a less vulnerable category

Ecosystem a community of plants and animals that live together and that rely on each other and the same soil, air and water in order to survive

Endangered describes a species threatened with immediate extinction throughout all or most of its range

Environment the air, water, rocks, soil, wildlife and all other surroundings of a plant or animal at any one time

Extinct describes any species of plant or animal no longer known to exist anywhere

Extirpated describes a species known to exist in the wild, but not in a country it previously inhabited

Habitat describes the natural environment of an animal or plant

Natural resources living and non-living parts of the natural environment that are or may be useful to people

PCB an industrial chemical. Its full name is polychlorinated biphenyl

Population groups of any one kind of plant or animal

Species a distinct kind of animal or plant, such as a mallard duck or a green frog, that mates and has young with another of its kind

Survive to continue to live and have young despite problems

Threatened describes a species likely to become endangered in the near future

Vulnerable a species at risk of becoming threatened

Wildlife describes all native animals and plants living in the wild

INDEX

acid rain, 64–67, 84, 85, 89, 90
acid shock, 65
activities,
    adopt a tree, 59
    build a bird house, 84
    build a rainforest tree, 73
    experience wilderness, 46
    make a crane egg, 36
    make a rainforest breakfast, 74
    monitor acid rain, 90
    plant a prairie, 53
    test for acid rain, 67, 90
    test fright distance, 51
    watch an oil invasion, 61
    See also fund-raising, games, kids
    in action, lifestyle
Alaska, 43, 60, 69, 90
alligators, 23
Amazon, 75–76
angonokas, 31
Aransas Wildlife Refuge, 34, 35
Arctic, 33, 68
Audubon, 30, 37
auks, great, 17

bacteria, 63, 66
baleen, 20
bamboo, 48, 49
BARK, 90
barley, 10
bats, bumblebee, 31
batteries, 29, 63, 83
Bay of Fundy, 21
bears,
    grizzly, 47, 52, 60
    polar, 23
Belize, 77
bioindicators, 13, 67
biological diversity, 9, 72
biologists, 40, 90
bison,
    plains, 52
    wood, 55
blue jays, 49

bluebirds, Eastern, 14, 15, 55
bobcats, 46
Brazil, 76, 77
bromeliads, 72
butterflies, Queen Alexandra's
    Birdwing, 31

cacti, 23
Canada, 8, 14, 26, 27, 33, 34, 38, 39,
    42, 43, 47, 52–55, 69, 78, 80
canaries, miner's, 13
caribou,
    barren ground, 32
    woodland, 17
carnivores, 46, 47
cars, 9, 61, 66, 68, 69, 85. *See also*
    roads
cassavas, 10
cats, 24, 43, 46, 79
Central America, 27, 71
chickens, greater prairie, 52
China, 48, 49
cicadas, 58
clams, 13, 61
Clean Air Act, 66, 67
clear-cut, 57, 58, 75
climate, 17, 69
collar-bands, 41, 49
compost, 54, 83, 84
condors, California, 31
conifers, 46
conservation, 14, 24, 37, 52, 77, 79
containers, returnable, 82
corals, 23
cormorants, 61
corn, 10, 52, 74
coyotes, 40, 46, 47
crabs, 61
cranes,
    sandhill, 35, 37, 39
    whooping, 34–41
crocodiles, 22

crops,
    cereals, 74
    rainforest, 70–77, 91
    rotation, 54
cucumber trees, 14
curlews, Eskimo, 14, 31, 55

daisies, 49
DDT, 15, 27, 63
deer, 22, 68
delisted, 14, 15
destruction. *See* habitats
dinosaurs, 16
disposal, 29, 83
diversity, 9, 72
dodo,
    birds, 11, 12, 14
    trees, 11
dolphins, 63
down-listed, 14
dragonflies, 72
drugs,
    aspirin, 10
    digitalis, 10
    rainforest, 75
ducks, 13, 21, 54, 55, 64

eagles, 27, 60, 89
ebony trees, 14, 23, 71
ecosystems, 11
Ecuador, 71, 74, 77
eggs, 26–27, 34, 36–37, 61, 65, 72
elephants, African, 22, 24, 25
endangered, 8, 9, 14–16, 18, 21, 22,
    24, 29, 34, 42–43, 46, 50, 52, 54,
    55, 58, 71, 81, 82, 85, 86, 88–91
endangered species,
    list, 14, 15, 54, 55
    trade, 24, 25
energy, 61, 66, 84, 85
    wildlife-friendly use, 66, 84–85
environment, 82–85, 88–90
Ethiopia, 74

extinction,
    accelerated, 14, 16, 17, 26, 29–31,
        34, 38, 42–43
    commercial, 20–21
    natural, 16, 17
extirpated, 14, 52, 55
Exxon Valdez, 43, 60, 61

falcons, peregrine, 26–29, 55, 90
farming, 8, 9, 11, 15, 26, 35, 46–48,
    50, 52, 54, 71, 74, 80–82
fertilizers, 54, 63, 84
fish, 15, 17, 23, 27, 47, 55, 61, 63–66,
    80
    tropical, 23
fishing, 17, 43, 63, 78, 80
food chains, 26
forests, 48–50, 56–59, 68–77, 85, 89
    old growth, 56, 58, 59
fossils, 16, 84
foxes, 13, 14, 40, 52, 90
foxgloves, 10, 11
frogs, 65
    arrow poison, 71, 72
    green, 64
    leopard, 49
fuels, fossil, 84, 85
fund-raising,
    art shows, 90–91
    bake sales, 76–77
    grocery store tapes, 76
    plant sales, 76

games,
    pesticide chain reaction, 28–29
    raisins and extinction, 16
garbage, wildlife and, 29, 55, 85, 87
gardens, wildlife-friendly, 84
geese, 54, 64
global warming, 68
golf courses, 50
gophers, 15, 55
governments, 14, 39, 42, 43, 48, 77,
    83, 89
grasses, 53
grasslands, 8, 52
Gray's Lake National Wildlife
    Refuge, 39

greenhouse effect, 63, 68, 69, 75, 84,
    90
group projects, 76–77, 86–91.
    See also activities, fund-raising,
    games, kids in action
Guelph University, 21

habitats, 8, 9, 15, 37, 38, 45, 46–48,
    52–55, 57, 58, 60, 61, 69, 75,
    81–86, 90
hares, snowshoe, 58, 59
hogs, pygmy, 31
hummingbirds, 33, 84
hunting, 8, 14, 17, 18, 20, 21, 24, 25,
    30–35, 38, 42, 43, 47, 48, 54, 78

Iceland, 17
incinerators, 62, 83
India, 43
Indonesia, 74
insecticides, 15, 61
ivory, 23, 25, 88

jaguars, 21, 70
Japan, 43
jellyfish, 63, 80

kids in action, 78–91
    adopt a tree, 59
    feed the birds, 33
    patrol for pesticides, 29
    plant tall-grass prairie, 53
    protest in public, 25
    recycle paper, 56
    save cranes' feeding area, 37
    save seabirds, 78
    say no to Styrofoam, 69
    write letters, 75, 89
krill, 20
Kuyt, Ernie, 40–41

Labrador, 80
lemmings, 33
leopards, 22
leukaemia, 75
lifestyle,
    wildlife-friendly, 82–85, 87
logging, 57, 58, 71, 72

loons, 64
louseworts, Furbish's, 79
lynx, 58, 59

mahogany, 70, 72
Malaysia, 70, 80
Manitoba, 52, 53
mastodons, 17
metals, 13, 65, 82, 83, 85
Mexico, 77
migration, 34, 35, 38, 39, 41
minks, sea, 14, 21
monkeys, woolly spider, 31
moose, 17, 68
mosquitoes, 11, 12, 27, 46, 72
murrelets, marbled, 58
murres, 60
muskoxen, 42
mussels, 61

National Audubon Society, 37
nests, 15, 17, 26, 30, 31, 34, 36,
    38–41, 49, 50, 54, 70, 80
nets, drifting, 63
newspapers, 88, 89
North America, 34, 37, 47, 56, 58

oceans, 17, 43, 55, 60, 61, 63, 69
ocelots, 23
oil,
    spills, 43, 60–63, 90
    tankers, 60, 61, 85
Operation Tiger, 43
orchids, 23
orioles, 70
ospreys, 27
otters, sea, 43, 60, 61
owls,
    burrowing, 15, 54, 55, 90
    snowy, 33

Pacific Ocean, 43, 58
packaging, 72, 82, 85
Panama, 70, 75
pandas, giant, 31, 48–49
panthers, Florida, 79
pelicans, white, 14, 15, 35
periwinkles, rosy, 75

Peru, 77
pesticides, 8, 9, 15, 26–29, 54, 82–84
pigeons, passenger, 9, 30, 31
pine martens, Newfoundland, 58
plankton, 20, 60
plovers, 26, 55
poachers, 24, 25
poisoning, 8, 13, 15, 18, 26–27, 47, 49, 54, 55, 60–61, 65
pollution, 8, 35, 61, 63, 66, 69, 75, 78, 83, 85, 89
    air, 8, 35, 66, 75, 83, 85
    water, 60–61, 63, 66, 83, 85, 89
potatoes, 10, 11
prairie,
    aspen, 52, 54
    fescue, 52, 54
    mixed, 52, 54
    short-grass, 54
    tall-grass, 52–54, 85
press coverage, 25, 86, 88
Puerto Rico, 81

raccoons, 48, 49
radio, 21, 49, 84, 87, 88
rainforests,
    Costa Rican, 71, 76, 77, 80
    foods, 74
    fund-raising, 90, 91
    Malaysian, 71
    medicines, 75
    weather, 75
    write for, 75
rare, 22–23, 25, 47, 52. *See also* vulnerable
recycling,
    paper, 56, 76, 82, 83
    reforestation, 59
rhinoceros, 24, 31, 88
rice, 10, 74, 77
roads, 34, 48, 50, 52, 57, 71
rose, prairie, 15

salamanders, 65
salmon, 47, 61
Saskatchewan, 35, 86
sculpins, 15, 55

seals,
    Mediterranean monk, 21, 31
    northern fur, 63
seed dispersal, 11, 13, 24
sewage, 63
shipping, 21, 63
shopping,
    rainforest-friendly, 72
    take-out treats, 85
    wildlife-friendly, 82
snakes,
    Malayan pit viper, 10
    timber rattlesnake, 49
soil, 13, 32, 49, 52–54, 57, 65, 71, 83
South America, 27, 71, 75
squirrels, 56, 69
St. Lawrence River, 21, 63
storms, 15, 35
Styrofoam, 9, 68, 69
sustainable numbers, 30–32
swallows, 15, 70
swamps, 17, 40, 49, 50, 54, 55, 81
sweet potatoes, 10
Switzerland, 25

tanagers, 70
teak, 23, 71, 72
Texas, 34, 35, 40, 41, 52
threatened, 11, 14, 15, 18, 27, 43, 50, 54, 55, 57, 58, 78, 79
tigers,
    Indian, 9, 43
    saber-toothed, 16
toads, 65
    golden, 31
    Puerto Rican crested, 81
tortoises,
    Madagascar land, 31
    shell, 22
toxic waste, 29, 62, 83
transportation, wildlife-friendly, 85
trilobites, 16
trout, brook, 49
tubocurarine, 75
tundra, 32, 33
turtles,
    leatherback, 80
    sea, 63

    snapping, 25, 64
    wax, 22
tusks. *See* ivory

United Nations, 47, 69
United States, 8, 33, 38, 55

violets, African, 31
vipers, Malayan pit, 10
vulnerable, 14–16, 54, 55

waste, reduction, 56, 83, 87
wetlands, 54, 55
whales,
    beluga, 63, 90
    blue, 21, 91
    bowhead, 21, 90
    grey, 20, 60
    humpback, 15, 21
    right, 9, 20, 21, 31
wheat, 10, 52
wilderness, 34, 45, 46, 47, 49, 57
Winnipeg, 53
wolverines, 46, 47, 90
wolves, 32, 42
Wood Buffalo National Park, 34, 35, 39, 40
Workers For Wildlife, 9, 81
World Wildlife Fund, 9, 21, 25, 27, 37, 43, 49, 76, 77, 78, 81, 89, 90, 91
wrens, house, 15

Yemen, 25

zero-tillage, 54

ANSWERS

Spot the wildlife products, page 22
1.Leopard skin coat, 2.American crocodile purse, 3.Himalayan musk deer perfume, 4.Hawkbill turtle wax, 5.Ocelot pet, 6.Indian python cowboy boots, 7.Geometric tortoise shell glasses, 8.Artichoke cactus, Tobusch fishhook cactus, black lace cactus garden, 9.Black coral necklace, 10.Ebony chopsticks, 11.Chinese alligator shoes, 12.Teak table, 13.Black rhinoceros trophy head, 14.African elephant ivory piano keys, 15.Bald eagle feather boa, 16.Paradise parakeet pet, 17.Various African freshwater tropical fish pets, 18.Polar bear rug, 19.Asian elephant foot umbrella stand, 20.Wild orchid plants.

Survival school, page 49
Blue jays love city parks and areas with oak trees.

Leopard frogs would have a tough time surviving. City water is scarce and what there is of it contains chemicals and purifiers that would harm the frogs.

Timber rattlesnakes won't survive in a city suburb. There are no caves available and even if there were, people would search them out and kill them. Because they can't survive near people, timber rattlesnakes are extinct in Canada and in trouble in the U.S.

Common daisies flourish in bulldozed lots in suburbs.

Brook trout wouldn't survive: city water is low in oxygen and too silty.

Acid rain — the silent killer, page 64
Muskrat mounds provide homes for (1) muskrats and nesting sites for (2) Canada geese. (3) Loons dive for food. (4) A human fishes for dinner too. (5) Rushes and (6) lilies provide shelter for reptiles and amphibians such as (7) green frogs and (8) snapping turtles. (9) Water snakes zigzag over the water, snatching at (10) striders. (11) A green heron stands stock-still eyeing its next meal, a frog.

Below the surface live many kinds of fish. (12) Small mouthed bass, (13) common shiners, (14) yellow perch and (15) rainbow trout in all sizes mean the lake is healthy and the fish are reproducing every year.

The murky mud at the bottom teems with life. There are (16), beetles, (17) newts, (18) crayfish (19) snails, (20) tadpoles and zillions of microscopic creatures.

Acid Rain Witches' Brew, page 66
Here are some energy-saving ideas. How many others can you think of?
1.Ride your bike, take a bus or walk instead of getting a drive in a car. 2.Have to get a drive in a car? Try to arrange to car-pool with friends. 3.When you're out in the car, help to plan your trip so that your family does as many errands as possible and makes maximum use of the car. 4.Turn off the lights, stereo, TV, computer, etc., when you leave a room. 5.When it's cold outside, turn down the thermostat at home and put on another sweater. 6.Encourage your parents to buy energy-efficient, lower-wattage light bulbs. 7.Use as little air conditioning as possible — at home or in the car. 8.Go for a walk or a hike instead of playing a computer game. 9.Try canoeing in the summer instead of always using a motorboat..10.If your family decorates your house with coloured lights during the winter holidays, be sure to turn the lights off instead of leaving them on all night.

Temperature rising, page 68
Black spruce are not likely to survive. You'd think that their ability to hold water would help them in a dry, desert-like climate. But the bogs would likely dry up and black spruce would have no water source.

Moose are not likely to survive. In a desert-like climate, moose would have trouble finding water plants essential to their diet. Besides warmer temperatures, there is the added threat that deer may move north into moose country, bringing the fatal moose disease.

Red squirrels will likely survive. If the climate warms, grey squirrels may move into red squirrel territory, but red squirrels have already adapted to life with them.

The least weasel might survive. As long as the climate doesn't get too warm and there is still snow for tunnelling, this weasel can probably live as it does now. However, bigger weasels adapted to more southern climates may move in and push out the least weasel.

Wildlife close-up: The rainforest, page 70
The animals are (clockwise from top left): oriole, sloth, bat, frog, beetle, javelina (wild boar), tarantula, ants, jaguar.